HARRISBURG

The dome of the current capitol
has crowned Harrisburg since
the building was dedicated
in 1906.

An Illustrated History of Greater

HARRISBURG

LIFE BY THE MOVING ROAD

By

MICHAEL BARTON

PICTORIAL RESEARCH BY IRWIN RICHMAN

AND JOHN BECK

AMERICAN HISTORICAL PRESS

SUN VALLEY, CALIFORNIA

Library of Congress Catalogue Card Number: 2009935128

ISBN: 9780-965547-54-3

Bibliography: p. 217
Includes Index

DEDICATION

To Paul B. Beers

He out-wrote all of us.

And to Eric Ledell Smith

He had more to write.

Ralph Trembly derived this hand-colored lithograph of the burning of John Harris from the late-19th century painting by Benjamin R. Reeder, who borrowed heavily from Benjamin West's famous 1771 painting "Penn's Treaty with the Indians" for the composition. Courtesy, The Historical Society of Dauphin County, John Harris/Simon Cameron Mansion Museum

CONTENTS

Mechanics Bank
Dauphin Bank
Harris Mansion & Grave
Penns
VIEW OF

This "View of Harrisburg, Penn." dates from 1855 and was "Drawn on Stone from Nature and The Daguerreotype by J.T. Williams, York, Pa." During the pre-Civil War period many American cities received the "bird's eye" treatment by American artists and publishers. Vignettes around the borders of this large format (35" x 23") graphic show notable buildings, most of which are now destroyed or altered beyond recognition. (HSDC)

PREFACE

This latest revised edition of *Life by the Moving Road* sits at the end of a shelf full of history books written about Harrisburg. The first history of Dauphin County, in fact, a multi-county history, was written by I. Daniel Rupp in 1846 and is fortunately still available as a reprint. George Morgan's *Annals of Harrisburg*—actually, *Annals, Comprising Memoirs, Incidents and Statistics of Harrisburg, From the Period of its First Settlement. For the Past, the Present, and the Future*—we can call the first history of the city itself. Published in 1858, it consisted of just what its long title says. Morgan was followed in 1883 by Dr. William Henry Egle, inveterate, and sometimes debatable, recorder of the city's history. His multi-volumed works are still a unique resource. After Egle came Luther Reily Kelker's three-volume county history, in 1907. These tomes are so well known among local historians that we just call them "Egle" and "Kelker" for short.

The modern popular histories of Harrisburg prove by their sales that we still have a citizenry eager for history. Marian Inglewood (*Then and Now in Harrisburg*, 1925), George Donehoo (*Harrisburg, The City Beautiful, Romantic, and Historic*, 1927), and Paul B. Beers (*Profiles from the Susquehanna Valley*, 1973) informed local residents about their past through books and thousands of newspaper columns. Beers has been especially well-known as a journalist-historian. Until recently we could read the late Mary O. Bradley's "Cornerstone" articles in the *Patriot-News*. The late John Yetter's *Steelton, Pennsylvania: Stop, Look, Listen* (1979) is an insider's heartfelt history of the steel mill and its community. Ken Frew has written well-received essays for Historic Harrisburg's newsletter, and we look forward to his nearly completed book on the history of the city's architects and architecture. The late Ernest Morrison was an industrious historian of the State Hospital and an invaluable biographer of J. Horace McFarland. Photographic histories of Harrisburg, by Linda Ries, and of Hershey, by Mary Houts, both published by Arcadia, have been useful best sellers.

The Greater Harrisburg Area has recently received the attention it deserves from academic historians. The late Robert Grant Crist's *Camp Hill: A History* (1984) was the work of a West Shore native who was both an active citizen and a scholar. Prof. Gerald G. Eggert's *Harrisburg Industrializes: The Coming of Factories to an American Community* (1993) is the most substantial scholarship we have on the city's industrial past and its leaders. The eminent Prof. John Bodnar wrote *Steelton: Immigration and Industrialization, 1870-1940* (1977) while he was with the Pennsylvania Historical and Museum Commission. He shows what can be done with the local history of race and ethnicity. *Steelton* (Arcadia, 2008), put together by Prof. Simon Bronner and myself, interprets John Yetter's photographs as a visual history of that industrial village. *Harrisburg's Old Eighth Ward* (Arcadia, 2002), edited by myself and Jessica Dorman, reprints and analyzes J. Howard Wert's 1912-1913 newspaper articles about the most notorious and diverse neighborhood in the city. More studies are in the works now, including websites designed by my Penn State Harrisburg students dealing with the city's old 8th ward, the McCormick family, and the antebellum journals of attorney Charles Rawn.

Where does *Life by the Moving Road* fit? It's not simply a coffee-table book, but neither is it something that a professor would typically have written. This is an in-between book, hard to classify. I called it "written snapshots" the first time it was published, and I still think that's a useful description. I describe scenes and events that I think reveal city life over time.

This edition of my book has new chapters on the city's latest developments. Building on the previous selections of Irwin Richman, I have also found some new images for the book in the photographic collections of the Historical Society of Dauphin County. Kathryn McCorkle, its Executive Director, and Steven Bachmann, Curator, were perfectly generous with their assistance. Jeb Stuart, who works daily with Harrisburg history, was kind enough to provide photographs and a Foreword that sketches the city government's contributions to history. All of us are grateful for the historical journalism of Paul B. Beers and the scholarship of the late Eric Ledell Smith, and this book is dedicated to both of them. Finally, as I've said before, I'm most grateful to Harrisburg, for providing memorable stories and manifold readers.

FOREWORD

Many of us who live here in Harrisburg realize (and celebrate) the unusual degree to which we share our town with others.

A town of transplants and interlopers, as most political towns are, Harrisburg's oldtimers and natives graciously share the city—its institutions, its opportunties and its pockets of power—with newcomers. And increasingly, we locals are sharing Harrisburg with large groups of visitors and tourists, for whom our town is now an attractive destination. Imagine that!

In the current era of Mayor Steve Reed, the realization has spread that Harrisburg is a metropolis, the hub of a region. As a result, cityfolk, suburbanites and countryfolk share in the pleasures (sports, entertainment, business opportunity) of a big metropolis as well as its challenges (traffic, social responsibility, etc.), and, yes, we're doing a pretty good job of it.

As a state capital, we share Harrisburg with all Pennsylvanians. What we do here matters to them. Harrisburg belongs to them, as well as to us.

And, as "the home of the world's oldest democracy," that uninterrupted institution established by William Penn in 1682, and headquartered here since 1811, Harrisburg is a citadel of participatory government which Penn foresaw as "an example to the nations." Thus, we share Penn's legacy with all humanity, including those for whom democracy is still a dream.

We are proud of our heritage, here on the shores of the spectacular Susquehanna, where John Harris chose the intersection of two ancient Indian trails as the spot for his trading post and ferry service.

We are a history-minded community, with an abundance of history to share. Those who have witnessed even common-place episodes of history are quick and eager to share them. Our history is shared in the telling of tales, in the saving of artifacts, in the merchandising of memorabilia.

Many realize that our local history is the connection we share with generations past and generations yet to come. We are temporary stewards of Harrisburg heritage. Future generations only will have the pleasure of sharing what we preserve and pass on to them.

Our landmarks, our institutions, our memories, our magnificent waterfront, our quality of life—wouldn't it be a tragedy if these were not here for future Harrisburgers to share?

Books are a treasured and traditional medium through which history is shared. Many fascinating books—though hard to find today—have been written about Harrisburg. Professor Michael Barton, who shares history, in a most entertaining way, as raconteur, lecturer and author, produced *Life by the Moving Road*, in 1983. Our enthusiasm for local history made it a sell-out and, ultimately, a collector's item. Fifteen years later, we enthusiatically welcome this brilliantly updated edition!

David J. Morrison,
Executive Director,
Historic Harrisburg Association

Troops from Harrisburg gathered at Camp Boas before seeing action during the Civil War. (HSDC)

This Taufshein, a birth and baptismal certificate, is a fine example of the Fraktur used by the Pennsylvania German population in the 18th and 19th centuries.

EPIGRAPH

"I beg your pardon," said the Mole, pulling himself together with an effort. "You must think me very rude, but all this is so new to me. So—this—is—a—River!"

"*The* River," corrected the Rat.

"And you really live by the river? What a jolly life!"

"By it and with it and on it and in it," said the Rat. "It's brother and sister to me, and aunts, and company, and food and drink, and (naturally) washing. It's my world, and I don't want any other. What it hasn't got is not worth having, and what it doesn't know is not worth knowing. Lord! the times we've had together!"

Kenneth Grahame
The Wind in the Willows

By the early 1840s, when this lithograph was made,
Harrisburg had become a thriving river port. It was the capital
of the Commonwealth of Pennsylvania; it boasted that great
engineering marvel of its day, the Camelback Bridge; and it
had already become an important rail center. (HSDC)

Right: Barges carried coal for Harrisburg down the
Susquehanna from nearby mines to be unloaded at Front
Street, shown here. Much coal was lost overboard along the
way, and, until the 1960s, barges salvaging coal from the
river bottom were a common sight. (HSDC)

I
THE MOVING ROAD THAT USED TO BE

Gertrude Stein's charge against Oakland, California—"There's no there there"—cannot be put to Greater Harrisburg. There's a here *here, a feeling for place come from custom and geography. The literal core of our history and the sense of "here" is the Susquehanna River, and so it is important to know how the city's river was used in the past. But it is even more important to know that this is still the river's city.*

The Great Valley of the Appalachian Mountains runs up from Alabama and across to Newfoundland. The narrow valley of the Susquehanna River goes down from New York to Chesapeake Bay. In southeastern Pennsylvania these valleys cross paths, and there is Greater Harrisburg, on the shores of the Susquehanna River, where the Cumberland part of the Great Valley from the west meets the Lebanon part of the Great Valley from the east. Trains, boats, ferries, canals, bridges, roads, and people all wind up knotted here, where the elder John Harris, without a bird's eye view, simply found a good spot to ford the river and sell some lots.

There is only one drawback to this convenient geography. The Susquehanna drains all the central part of Pennsylvania. Because this central part is hilly, the river receives all the rain water quickly and melting snow eventually. When the river freezes in the Winter, ice floes can also jam it in the Spring. It would be difficult to find a river more likely to overflow, and, since Harrisburg lies below its major feeding branches, a city more likely to flood.

The first recorded major flood was in 1744, the second in 1758, then 1772, 1784, 1786 (when the overflow left pumpkins from upstream all over), 1800, 1814, 1817, 1846 (when Camelback Bridge was half destroyed), 1865, 1889 (the first well-documented disaster), 1894, 1902 (when Camelback Bridge was finally destroyed), 1904, 1921, 1936 (the second worst), 1972 (the very worst), and 1975. Actually, these are only the floods mentioned most often. There have been more than 40 in the last 200 years.

We can tell from reading the diary of Mrs. Sallie Simonton that when you have felt one flood, you have felt them all. Her description seems close to what we ourselves might describe:

March 16th, 17th, 18th, 1865. Never since we became friends, and that is a long time ago, even so far back as I can remember, for I was born and raised on its banks, have I seen our usually placid river rise in such bold and defiant might as during the three days above named. The spring freshet . . . came upon us in all its devastating power. The bank was daily thronged with people, who with no little interest watched and waited to see if the old railroad bridge would give way before the mighty current of swollen waters as they lashed against its side. Almost contrary to our most sanguine expectations, with the aid of ropes and iron stays, it passed safely through the crisis, its battered sides bearing witness to the severity of the contest. Good for you old bridge. . . . Meanwhile, the waters

The flood of 1889 left the Camelback Bridge only somewhat intact, as can be seen in this photograph taken from the Cumberland County end of the bridge, on the west shore opposite Harrisburg. (HSDC)

Above: *The second worst flood to hit Harrisburg was that of March 1936. Shipoke is to the right, beyond the Reading Railroad Bridge. The photographer's boat was evidently stationed directly in front of the John Harris mansion. (HSDC)*

Left: *The Camelback Bridge endured for so many years and survived so much abuse because it was an elaborate and craftily engineered wooden structure. The beams, joists, and supports were all made big to withstand shock, and assembled so that individual members could easily be replaced when they began to decay. (HSDC)*

The Kelso Ferry House, on the West Shore near the Cumberland Valley Railroad Bridge, was built in 1734 and was used by ferry masters in the pre-bridge era. (HSDC)

began to creep stealthily over our nice green ward, laying waste trees, fences, etc., coming nearer and nearer even into our very abodes, taking lordly possession and shoving out the lawful owners. What was once terra firma became a waste of waters navigable by small craft. Here and there were to be seen some half dozen heads peering out of the top-most story of a dwelling while beneath was a little barge unloading its contents of bread and food for the hungry inmates. . . . At this juncture of affairs, river, canal, and creek united in forming one vast sea of water; . . . For three days we lived on an island, holding no communication with the outer world around us, every avenue of ingress and egress being closed. No water, no gas, the works for the time being submerged, we were in fact transported to primitive times and made to realize the difference between the convenience of the present and the inconveniences of the past.

Otherwise, life on the moving road is not what is used to be. The river used to carry cargo. An early historian, J.P. Keller, wrote that in Spring, 1827, exactly 1,631 rafts, 1,370 arks, and about 300 keelboats ("broadhorns") passed Harrisburg. The rafts were trees lashed together, bound for lumber yards; the arks and broadhorns carried coal, flour, whiskey, and wheat. Another historian, the Reverend Silas

Swallow, writing in 1915, said one time he saw 20 lumber rafts on the river while he stood in one spot. The great rafts were 150 or 300 feet long, made of trees 25 to 80 feet long. The rafts were not more than 25 feet wide, in order to pass through the channels and rapids. Later, cargo used to be gotten from the river itself, as coal dredgers would scrape "black diamonds" from the bottom.

Steamboats used to be on the river. In 1825 three docked at Harrisburg on their way north. In 1826 one of them, the *Susquehanna*, exploded, and steamboating fizzled. Only the Millersburg ferry remains to remind us of the riverine travel.

The river used to be a place for grand fun. Hundreds of children would swim in it every summer day off City Island. Scores of rowboats and canoes used to be launched from private moorings or boat clubs along both banks. A large and popular dance floor used to be anchored in the river where a fellow, if he had a striped blazer and a straw skim-mer, would take his gal and her chaperone for a date. There his corseted sweetheart could admire him for winning the single sculls race that afternoon, or for captaining the first-place crew.

They used to tell some good stories about the river. Reverend Swallow told two of them to the Historical Society of Dauphin County. They were about the men who worked the river.

The raftsmen were jolly crews not always mindful of others' rights, and by no means sticklers for the golden rule. . . . four jolly but hungry raftsmen asked a good house wife to sell them bread and pastry. She browbeat them as thieves, and they, intent on being what she trusted them to be, put two fence rails under her clay-formed garden oven and carried it and its half baked bread, pies and cakes to the raft, and then floated; meanwhile watching the contents of the oven that they might not get too well done. They feasted for two or three days. In their tramp return, two

As late as 1901, log rafts continued to float past the city. Within a few years, they too would be gone, and the Susquehanna would become an almost functionless presence in the life of the city. (HSDC)

A low river level, as in this photo from about 1900, was certainly less destructive than a flood, but it still created many problems for Harrisburg residents. (HSDC)

The statewide canal system was an engineering wonder of 19th-century Pennsylvania. The canals carried both travelers and commercial goods until the 1920s. Traces of the canal bed and the towpath are still visible around Harrisburg. (HSDC)

The Pennsylvania Canal and towpath, pictured here at the Dauphin Narrows about 1900, was then a major artery of transportation. The common mode of transportation has changed, however, and this site today is paved over to accomodate trucks and automobiles on Route 22. (HSDC)

weeks afterward, toward their home a hundred miles further north, they stopped and paid the good lady for the oven and its contents, and then tramped on northward. Ever after, it is said, she spoke well of the river men.

All the raftsmen of that period knew a pilot known as "Uncle Ben." Some of his descendants live in the vicinity of Harrisburg now. He was a logician of the practical type. A fellow worker steered the raft on which they were floating within a foot of a rock, and when Uncle Ben, the pilot, chided him for so close a call, he excused himself by saying, "a miss is as good as a mile." Uncle Ben dissented and they came near to blows in the hour's argument that followed. Next morning when the steersman awoke, laying on the raft with only a horse blanket for a bed, he was in a rage because someone while he slept had placed a putrid fish within an inch of his nose and he had been smelling the odor all night. Uncle Ben condoled with him, but this time chided him for ill temper, since "a miss is as good as a mile," and the fish had not touched his nose. Thereafter that particular raft was steered as far as possible from danger.

Today the old gritty uses of the river are dried up, the stories have stopped, and there is less playing in it. Since the city built a retaining wall of steps and the Dock Street dam down by Shipoke, it looks different—no more puddles and sand bars in the summer, or muddy, littered shorelines in the Spring. The water is now mainly a place for some bass fishing, power boating, and man drowning. While the river used to be, literally, part of our ancestors (they drank it until the city found a new source for water), and our ancestors used to be, literally, part of the river (it took all the city's sewage), now our sodality is only aesthetic. The ornamental Susquehanna lolls by, and we look at it, or jog along it. But each year we fear that Sallie's friend may still astonish.

Sinclair's lithograph of the attempted burning of John Harris certainly does not suggest that his assailants were intoxicated. In fact, the Indians appear quite soberly purposeful. Nor does the picture give any hint that Harris will shortly be dramatically rescued. (HSDC)

II
THE ATTEMPTED HISTORY OF JOHN HARRIS' BURNING

In 1733 America was a land of little villages. Of its nearly half million citizens, only 12,000 lived in Boston, 10,000 in Philadelphia, and 7,000 in New York (a city then merely twice the size of Charleston, South Carolina and Newport, Rhode Island). The rest of the world was larger in every way: in 1720, when six patients in Boston died from smallpox innoculations, 60,000 in Marseilles died from Bubonic plague, and 300,000 in Calcutta would soon die in an earthquake and wind storm.

By 1733 the elder John Harris had settled on the east shore of the Susquehanna River in south central Pennsylvania. Like other emigrants, he expected to escape those immense miseries of the Old World, and he also prefigured his ferry landing might become another peaceful and prosperous American village. So like earlier pioneers, such as New York's Peter Minuit and Philadelphia's William Penn, John Harris began to palaver and trade with the Indians. But in doing so, a particularly New World misery befell him—he was accosted by his customers. Their attempt to burn him is the first famous story of Greater Harrisburg's history. Many other white captives left written narratives of their adventure and internment, but Harris didn't, so his biographers and illustrators were able to retell and redraw the story, depending on the lessons they wanted to learn and then teach. Their search for a usable past is as interesting as what they thought they found.

One could call the elder John Harris a chicaning, gambling, slaveholding brewer. Or one could call him an inventive, foresighted, masterly pioneer. Call him both kinds of men at once or somebody in between them, but Harrisburg wants a history of its first settler, John Harris, and especially of his attempted burning by the Indians, and has had to settle for a story.

The story is a myth beyond the facts—"a belief embodying a visionary ideal"—since the mysterious establisher did not leave a detailed account of his actions or even his looks.

There has been no controversy about the ordinary facts of John Harris' life, so let us move right along to the most extraordinary "event" of his days at the ferry, paying close attention to the several versions of the story written by Harrisburg historians. The first version, in I. Daniel Rupp's *History of Dauphin County*, published in 1846, noted that the story of the attempted burning had "excited considerable interest" and had been the object of "much inquiry." Rupp's description of the event quotes from an account by George W. Harris, the first John Harris' great-grandson:

On one occasion, a band of Indians, who had been down the river, or as is said, to the East, on a trading excursion, came to his house. Some, or most of them, were intoxicated. They asked for lum, *meaning West India rum, as the modern whiskey was not then manufactured in Pennsylvania. Seeing they were already intoxicated, he feared mischief, if he gave them more; and he refused. They became enraged and seized him and tied him to the mulberry tree to burn him. Whilst they were proceeding to execute*

their purpose, he was released, after a struggle, by other Indians of the neighborhood, who generally came across the river. How the alarm was given to them, whether by firing a gun or otherwise, or by whom, is not now certainly known. In remembrance of this event, he afterwards directed that on his death he should be buried under the mulberry tree, which had been the scene of this adventure. Part of the trunk of this tree is still standing. It is ten feet up to the lowest limb, and the stump is eleven feet, six inches in circumference. The writer (G.W. Harris) of this has eaten mulberries from this tree, which was one of the largest of its species.

The second version of the assault, in George Morgan's *Annals of Harrisburg*, published 12 years later in 1858, shows plagiarism of Rupp:

. . . it happened one day that a number of Indians of the Mahanoy, Mahotongo or Shawanese tribe, (most probably the latter,) who had been down the river either on a predatory or trading expediton, stopped at the house of Mr. Harris on their return northward. Most, or all of them, were under the influence of liquor, and demanded of Mr. Harris an additional supply of lum, *meaning West India rum, as the modern whiskey was not then manufactured in the Province. Perceiving that they were already intoxicated, and fearing mischief, Mr. Harris refused to grant the demand; whereupon they became greatly exasperated and dragged him to an adjoining mulberry tree, to which they firmly bound him.*

And then Morgan worked on embellishment, adding much fuel to Harris' fire:

Here they declared their intention to

Left: *Relicwood was dearly loved by the 19th century. The root and slab are supposed to be pieces of the Mulberry Tree to which John Harris was tied. The gavel's silver band announces that it, too, was carved from the same sacred wood. Photo by Mark Dorfman (HSDC)*

Above: *This steel engraving from Dr. William H. Egle's* History of the County of Dauphin *(1883) is a curiosity in that it is identical with the anonymous watercolor shown on the back cover, except that Harris and all of the Indians (except for the innocuous group in the canoe) have been removed. Possibly the artist (or Dr. Egle) wanted to show a scene less frantic than the attempted burning and used the other picture as a source. (HSDC)*

torture and burn him alive, and bade him prepare for instant death. Dry wood was gathered and piled around his feet, and torches held in readiness to kindle it; the yells of the enraged savages echoed along the river shore and through the surrounding forest, while with demoniac gestures they danced around their victim. Death in its most cruel form was before him; and, bereft of hope, he gave himself up for lost. In vain he supplicated for mercy, and offered to give up everything in exchange for life; but the savages were deaf to his entreaties, and declared he should die. The flaming torch was advanced toward the pile, and about being applied, when a band of friendly Indians, supposed to have belonged to the Paxton tribe . . . burst suddenly upon the scene and set him at liberty.

The one new feature of Morgan's version is his introduction of a new character in the drama:

These Indians were led on by a negro man named "Hercules," a slave belonging to Mr. Harris, who at the first alarm ran to the neighboring tribe to beg for succor, and now brought it to his master's relief. The deliverance was well-timed. A moment's delay would have been fatal. The presence of mind, the decision, the speed of this negro alone saved Mr. Harris; and so sensible was he of the great service rendered to him by this poor slave that he instantly emancipated him, and some of the descendants of the worthy Hercules resided in the borough for a number of years, enjoying their freedom, so nobly won.

The rescue, wrote Morgan, was "a signal deliverance; it was a manifest evidence of God's merciful interposition," and Harris' grave by the mulberry tree was likewise "a momento at once of savage ebriety, domestic fidelity, and above all, of the watchfullness of Him 'who alone can inflict or withold the stroke of death'." These "facts" had been gathered from an account of the incident published in 1828 by the legislator Samuel Breck, who had heard them from Robert Harris, the grandson of the elder John Harris. Robert "had received them as part of the traditional history of his family." Morgan's argument for trusting the tale asked his readers, in effect, to believe any idea that could not be disproved:

As there has never been any documentary evidence to substantiate this exciting episode in the life of Mr. Harris, there are some disposed to consider it a myth; yet we might very properly ask, has there been anything adduced to disprove it? Tradition may err; but it strikes us that if it does in this case, it would not have remained over one hundred and thirty years without being discovered.

The distinctive feature of Morgan's account is that he has inserted Hercules into the rescue; Rupp, you will recall, had George Harris saying that no one knew for certain who had given the alarm. Morgan believed that Robert Harris' memory was accurate when he included Hercules in the story he told to Samuel Breck in 1828, but that Robert's memory "had become impaired by old age" when he later left Hercules out of the story he told to William S. Reeder in 1839. But Morgan's effort to patch this problem does not explain why Robert and George Harris' accounts seem to disagree on so vital a point as Hercules.

The third version of the story, in Dr. William Egle's *History of the County of Dauphin,* published in 1883, supplied as much corroborating evidence as Egle could still find. He began by admitting that there were "all sorts of versions" of the incident "and even doubts of its truthfulness." But Egle asserted that "It was no myth, this attempt to burn John Harris, and although the pen and pencil have joined in making there from a romance and heightened it with many a gaudy coloring, yet accurate resources have furnished us with the details here given." Egle revised Morgan's estimate that the "Shawanese" had assaulted Harris; in fact, Egle called them Harris' best allies and said they saved him from the raiding party, possibly of "Onondagoes." Egle's account of the event is otherwise brisk and not exceptional. His effort at substantiation took up more space than the re-telling of the attempted burning, and he even cited his own grandmother's testimony. Egle did add one new anecdote, however:

Mr. Maclay also furnished a statement, which he had heard from his mother, to the effect that some friends endeavored to dissuade the old gentleman, Mr. Harris, from his determination to be buried under the mulberry tree, alleging that the river bank was being washed away and the grave might be exposed and perhaps washed away, and that he ought to be buried in the Paxtang church graveyard, but that he silenced all argument by saying that if you bury me out in Paxtang, I'll get up and come back.

The fourth version, published in 1907, is hardly a variant. Luther

Reily Kelker wrote in the three-volume *History of Dauphin County,* that for "many of the facts herein given" about the attempted burning of Harris, he was "indebted to the late Dr. Egle." But Kelker understated his debt—every word of his four-page description comes straight from Egle's *History of the County of Dauphin,* excepting the last paragraph which Kelker wrote.

The fifth version first appeared in Marian Inglewood's "Then and Now in Harrisburg" column in the *Patriot;* it reappeared in her book of the same title published several months later, in 1925. The first "modern" cumulative version of the event, Inglewood's prose style is just efficiently plain, not ornately romantic. Here the Indians are dispossessed Native Americans, not passionate savages (they are not even "intoxicated"):

The Indians who lived here were in the main friends of Mr. Harris and the other settlers, although a band occasionally happened along who resented the intrusion of the white man and tried to make things unpleasant for him. Upon one such occasion a number of Indians whom Mr. Harris had unintentionally made angry by refusing to sell them "fire water," dragged the pioneer to a mulberry tree near the bank of the river, bound him hand and foot, and declared they were going to burn him alive.

Here Hercules is simply a timely rescuer, not a perfectly loyal and brave slave:

But just as the torch was about to be applied, a different kind of war whoop resounded through the forest, and a band of friendly Indians rushed forward, scattered the would-be torturers,

and set *John Harris free.*

Hercules, a negro slave who belonged to the Harris family, had hurried to a tribe on the western side of the river as soon as he saw the plight his master was in, and succeeded in bringing help just in the nick of time. A few minutes' longer delay would have been fatal.

It was almost a miraculous deliverance. Hercules was given his freedom at once as a reward for the part he played in the rescue. And as a reminder to every one how God had saved him that day, Mr. Harris said *that when he died he wanted to be buried under the mulberry tree where he came very nearly being tortured to death. His family tried to dissuade him from his purpose, and suggested the cemetery at the old Paxtang church as being far more fitting, but he told them bluntly if they buried him there he'd get up and walk back.*

In short, Inglewood and her audience were not Victorians. They did not have the same needs as Rupp, Morgan, Egle-Kelker, and

Tinian, *built about 1760 in present day Highspire, was the home of Colonel James Burd (1726-1798), one of Dauphin County's most influential citizens and a veteran of both the French and Indian, and the Revolutionary wars. Tinian, seen in this 1930 photo with the original stone partly exposed, is now much altered and covered with aluminum siding. (HSDC)*

Before the Revolution, John Harris built his mansion about 100 yards further from the riverbank than the site of his father's cabin and grave. Somewhat enlarged and Victorianized by Simon Cameron, the mansion is otherwise unchanged. The grave of John Harris sits surrounded by a small iron fence and shaded by a mulberry (but not the original mulberry, which perished of flood, Pennsylvania winters, and old age some years ago). (HSDC) From Art Work of Harrisburg *(Chicago: W.H. Parish Publishing Co., 1892)*

their readers. She treated the story as being entirely credible, and was happy to spice it with color and drama. But in her final analysis it is only "almost miraculous."

The sixth version, in Dr. George P. Donehoo's *Harrisburg, The City Beautiful, Romantic, and Historic,* published in 1927, is most striking for its insistence on the usefulness, if not the truthfulness, of the event. There are no new details in his version and no new documents cited; Donehoo confesses that he has "hunted in vain for some reference to this incident in the letters and other documents of the period, but has been unable to find any mention of it. The story, therefore . . . must rest entirely upon tradition." Then comes his final appeal to the jury:

. . . we "critical historians" sometimes do more harm than good when we do away with all of our interesting and beautiful traditions because we can find no documentary evidence to support them. . . . What good does it do to get rid of them? They may be but "traditions," but these traditions have through years or through the centuries become historic traditions, worthy of perpetuation because of the romance they contain and because of the lessons which they teach.

And these were the lessons Donehoo thought the tradition taught.

The story shows that John Harris was a man of conviction, that he did not love his trade more than he did what was right, even when so doing endangered his life; it also reveals the devotion of a colored slave to his master, who must have treated him kindly, or he would not have sought to release him, and it also reveals the oft-time forgotten fact that Indians, when friends of the white man, protected their white friends even against the members of their own race.

Let us, therefore, as Harrisburgers keep the "tradition" of John Harris and his mulberry tree, just as we, as Americans, keep the "tradition" of George Washington and his cherry tree. . . .

Perhaps Donehoo did not want the facts to get in the way of his "good story," for he might risk losing a pluperfectly glorious past, present, and purpose.

As if all the old descriptions and discussions had become too snarled, the seventh and eighth versions of the attempted history told Harris' story on its own terms quickly, and then looked for perspective and irony, two crucial parts of our own generation's historical sensibility. In Paul Beers' *Profiles from the Susquehanna Valley,* published in 1973, we find the suggestion that if Harris had not built his first house so near the river, then the railroad would have laid its tracks right where Riverfront Park is now. Then in Richard Steinmetz, Sr. and Robert Hoffsommer's *This Was Harrisburg,* published in 1976, we find the observation that "Harrisburg owes its existence to the faithful devotion of a black slave."

The point in retelling these versions of the Harris legend is to demonstrate that each generation retells its history to find a usable past. What one generation accepts, the next questions, and then the next one insists upon, and back and forth until the latest generation can only shrug. One wishes Hercules had left a version. The legend is that he was buried unceremoniously where Harrisburg Hospital now stands, or else near John Harris, or else. . . .

A visit by George Washington is long remembered by the cities that can claim such a distinction. His trip through Harrisburg in 1794 is etched in the memories of local historians. From Cirker, Dictionary of American Portraits *(Dover: 1967)*

III
GEORGE WASHINGTON AND THE START OF STOPPING BY

In the generation after independence was secured and the republic was established, American and European observers began to take a more analytical than astonished look at this country. Their purpose was to explain to themselves and their readers just exactly what kind of place, and idea, had just been invented in America. The observers' own invention was the travelogue—the visitor's commentary, the trip diary, the letter home—a new type of literature for a new civilization. The best ones are American classics: Alexis de Tocqueville's Democracy in America *(1835), Frances Trollope's* Domestic Manners of the Americans *(1832), Lewis and Clark's* Journals *(1814), Francis Grund's* Aristocracy in America *(1839), and Harriet Martineau's* Society in America *(1837). The hundreds of lesser ones are at least informative. In all these travel accounts the facts that townspeople might take for granted were revealing details for the travelers.*

Harrisburg was mentioned often in such accounts. Indeed, it had to be, because it was almost impossible to traverse Pennsylvania without travelling through Harrisburg. Nature funneled the westward movement this way, into the Great Valley and across the river, so that tens of millions of Americans can say, "Oh yes, I've been to Harrisburg. I was on my way to. . . ."

October 3, 1794:

Geogre Washington was almost more itinerant than President. It is almost embarrassing to say he stayed here overnight too. The President arrived in Harrisburg late the afternoon of October 3, 1794. He was on his way to Carlisle to take command of the troops who would quench the Whiskey Rebellion in western Pennsylvania. A. Boyd Hamilton, former President of the Historical Society of Dauphin County, wrote that Washington uncovered his head and stood up in his carriage while it rolled up Second from Paxton Street. The Burgesses met him at the southeast corner of Market Square. They spoke a "very carefully worded" greeting to him (they pledged their moral support toward stopping the rebellion, but said "our sphere of action is too limited to produce any important effects"), and Washington's reply "smoothed over many political differences," according to Hamilton (the President said the inhabitants of Harrisburg were "virtuous and enlightened men" and that he appreciated their support of the Constitution and their "zealous and efficient exercise" in "defense of the laws"). Neither side was full of candor—Hamilton guessed there were only five Federalists in a town of 875 residents to support the President.

Washington stood on a stone horse block to deliver his speech. His name and the date of his visit were later inscribed on it, and the block now serves the John Harris Mansion as a stepping stone to the porch. Hamilton said there were few details but much debate on where the President ate and slept that night (probably at the Jones House on the southeast corner of Market Square) and whether he drove his own coach across the Susquehanna or rode on Harris' ferry (in his diary Washington simply wrote, "forded the Susquehanna").

The 200th anniversary of Washington's birth, celebrated in 1932, was the occasion for local newspapers to reprint the story of his visit in all its glory, including the President's remark that he judged

While the claim to be the "oldest in the country" might be questioned, the Independence Island Rope Ferry, seen in this early 20th century postcard, was a survivor of a common 18th-century ferry type. Courtesy, Pennsylvania Historical and Museum Commission (PHMC)

Harrisburg "considerable" after he had dined and "walked through and around the town." When he departed on October 4, there was, according to Captain Samuel Dewees' diary, "great weeping and mourning," purportedly by the "women and children" who "covered" the "banks of the river on the town side," though it may have been the innkeeper Dewees heard in distress, since there is no record of Washington ever paying his bill.

What did other visitors say after stopping by Harrisburg in its early years? J.P. Keller, in a speech to the Historical Society of Dauphin County at the turn of the century, retrieved many reminiscences. The Reverend Manasseh Cutler, travelling through in 1787, said Harrisburg was "a beautiful town" containing about "one hundred houses" and "a great number of taverns" but "no churches yet." The people "appear well dressed, some gay," he wrote.

John Penn, a grandson of William Penn, said, in 1788, that the town's "situation," meaning its location, "is one of the finest I ever saw," but "Lebanon is infinitely larger."

About 1795 the Duke de la Rochefoucauld, touring America, said Harrisburg was more "compact" than Reading and had "a better appearance." Its "Germans and Irishmen" were "sensible and industrious," despite the "thirty-eight inns" compacted in town, a "number out of all proportion to that of Europe."

Miss Margaret Dwight, travelling from Connecticut to Ohio, stayed overnight in Harrisburg in 1810. She was not favorably impressed by the cockfight which took place at the tavern where she and her party

A visitor to Harrisburg in the late 18th or 19th century might have stayed at the Mermaid Tavern at the northwest corner of 2nd and Washington Streets. Early hotels tended to be primitive at best, and cautious travelers often arranged to stop in private homes. By 1906, the newly built Fox Hotel stood on the site of Mermaid Tavern. (HSDC)

slept. Neither was she pleased by the many "drunken, swearing wretches" she met: "A great many of the best young men of the town became so intoxicated that they could not get home unassisted," she testified. "Harrisburg is a very dissipated place I am sure," she concluded.

The 1819 diary of Ludwig Gall, offered recently in the *Pennsylvania Magazine of History and Biography* by Frederick Trautmann, tells a marvelous story about early Harrisburg. On August 30 Gall, trying to persuade other Germans to emigrate to America, wrote that "Harrisburg is one of those wonders that rise out of the wilderness and astonish Europeans . . . I know of no region of similar size, even along the Rhine, that surpasses the region around Harrisburg in extent, variety, and perfection of natural beauty." Such descriptions of the landscape and characterizations of the New World become repetitious in travellers' journals. But Gall's account of the contagious spirit of freedom in Harrisburg is unique. His bound ser-

Artists of all types and presidents are the best-remembered Harrisburg visitors. Shown here are: pianist Louis Moreau Gottschalk, singer Jenny Lind, and Presidents Lincoln, McKinley, Grant, and Roosevelt. From Cirker, Dictionary of American Portraits *(Dover: 1967)*

vant, whose passage to America Gall had paid, was becoming "coarser and more impudent" as he kowtowed to his master each day:

One morning, eight days after we arrived, he came half-drunk to me and, his hat on, spoke with unwonted familiarity. He knew the law in America, he said, and I had better realize he was my equal. If I didn't give him a seat at my table and a suit of Sunday clothes as good as mine, he was obliged to stay with me not an hour more. In fact he stayed less than an hour: I reprimanded him and he left and did not return. Although it had been in vain when my other servants had run away, I offered in English- and German-language newspapers a reward of $10 for the capture and return of this fellow, Peter Wissel by name. Next day he was delivered to me in the home of Justice of the Peace Mayer, in Harrisburg, by a neighborhood farmer. . . . Wissel repeated his assertion that he would return to me only on the condition that he eat at my table, as was the custom in this country. I had no choice therefore but to request that he be jailed until he promised to improve . . . Six weeks later the rascal wrote me that he would return to my service for two years if I would pay him $60 a year and cancel his debt to me, and if I expected him to return on any other terms, I must have no idea of life in an American jail. This message prompted me to inspect the jail. He was right: I had no idea of life in an American jail. I found him and eight of his ilk, in clean and decent clothes, sitting at a table in a big, airy, well-lighted room. On the table were newspapers, a bottle of whiskey, and of all things, playing cards—when gambling outside was against the law. . . . Methodists with a misplaced love of humanity supplied him and his fellows with an abundance

of food and drink. "You see for yourself," he said. "I want for nothing here. I have no reason to wish to live elsewhere." . . . In the end I had to let the fellow go. . . .

But Gall also found out later that Harrisburg was not all liberty and license in 1819:

Yet, the touted freedom of conscience notwithstanding, the prohibition on Sunday of work, hunting, dancing, and other amusements, and even music is strictly enforced. Indeed, I've been told, a Dutch physician, on the complaint of a neighbor, had to pay a fine of $4 because, ignorant of the law, he didn't stop on Sunday the musical clock he brought from Europe . . . I paid $4 because I worked a few minutes in my flower beds. My Neighbor was paid $2, in reward for his pious zeal. . .

That was what you found in Harrisburg if you stopped by in the early days—beauty, liberty, and propriety, or the land's, the man's, and the law's differing dignities. You found America.

A half-century after the Lochiel's heyday, the Commonwealth Hotel was the most luxurious place to stay in Harrisburg. The building was most likely erected in three stages by three different architects who felt that continuing the exact design of their predecessor would have shown a terrible lack of imagination. (HSDC) From Art Work of Harrisburg

"General" Mitchell (whose proper first name has been forgotten—if indeed he ever had another) was born into slavery in 1845, presumably not in Pennsylvania, which was a free state. He resided in Harrisburg from some time in the mid-19th century until his death early in the 1900s. He was regarded with respect and affection by all who knew him. (HSDC)

IV
THE FIRST CRUSADES

America's first age of reform came in the 1830s, after the Founding Fathers were gone and their progeny began striving to live up to them (Presidents John Adams and Thomas Jefferson brought that fact home when they both died on July 4, 1826). Andrew Jackson was President now, and provided the image, if not entirely the reality, that this would be the "era of the common man." The American Society for the Promotion of Temperance was organized in 1826. William Lloyd Garrison published the first issue of his abolitionist newspaper The Liberator *in 1831, and the American Anti-Slavery Society was founded in 1833 (nearly 200,000 Americans had joined anti-slavery societies by 1850). Oberlin College in Ohio, established in 1833, became the first college to admit both women and men, both white and black.* McGuffey's Readers, *thoroughly moralistic schoolbooks, were first published in 1836, the same year Massachusetts required children to attend school for at least three months a year, and the same year the Transcendental Club was formed in Boston. Its most prominent member, Ralph Waldo Emerson, announced, "What is man born for, but to be a reformer?" Ironically, neither Emerson nor his soul-mate, Henry David Thoreau, was ever very active in any reform movement.*

Greater Harrisburg's reformers were better organized. They worked against profanity, slavery, and whiskey, or at least promised they would.

Two weeks after New Year's, 1836, the Harrisburg Anti-Slavery Society was founded by about a hundred men and women. The Reverend Nathan Stem, Rector of St. Stephen's Episcopal Church, was elected President. Dr. William Rutherford, 31, physician and raccoon hunter, and Mordecai McKinney, 40, lawyer and defender of fugitive slaves, were Vice-Presidents. The Society's Corresponding Secretary was Samuel Cross, an Irish schoolteacher who "had faith in the efficacy of the two R's—Rattan and Ruler—to enforce the rules." (According to one anonymous historian, the schoolboys used to sing, "Cross by name and Cross by nature and Cross jumped out of an Irish potater.")

The founding was no convenient moral gesture practiced a comfortable distance from slavers. Harrisburg was a station on the Underground Railroad from Maryland to Canada, and the citizens had seen runaway slaves and abolitionists roughed up in town. On April 25, 1825, wrote one reporter: "a large crowd of colored men and boys made a desperate effort to take a poor fugitive slave from his owner and the officers of the law. They came streaming in hot haste... a tumultuous crowd." However, "they were unsuccessful in releasing the fugitive, and sixteen of the mob were arrested." Twelve were convicted, and 11 of those (one escaped) "went to the treadmill." In 1847 Frederick Douglass, the most famous ex-slave, and William Lloyd Garrison, the most famous abolitionist, held an anti-slavery rally at the Dauphin County Court House in Harrisburg. Both were abused by the crowd.

A safer crusade was the local temperance movement. But it is also more difficult to understand, for compared to the Constitution of the Harrisburg Anti-Slavery Society (the Preamble said, "our national existence is based on this principle, as recognized in the Declaration of Independence, that 'all mankind are created equal'"), what are we to make of the principles of Mr. C.

William Lloyd Garrison and Frederick Douglass came to Harrisburg in 1847 to hold an antislavery rally at the Dauphin County Courthouse. They were undaunted by the hostile reaction they received from much of the crowd. From Cirker, Dictionary of American Portraits *(Dover: 1967)*

Lewis, temperance lecturer at the Lochiel Church, who in 1869 urged:

Let our prating about social and political equalities have an end, and by our love for humanity, for ourselves and posterity, show that the first, highest and noblest equality within the reach of man's highest aspirations is—That all men should live soberly.

The Young Men's and Young Ladies'

Total Abstinence Society of Harrisburg was already active in 1840 when William R. Dewitt lectured in an unidentified local Presbyterian Church on "Profanity and Intemperance, Prevailing Evils." From his long "discourse," as he called it, we may read the following lines:

You often hear individuals exclaim . . . "Oh heavens! What a mistake!" "My Goodness! How you frighten me!" This is profanity.

There is no object in the Universe so disgusting as a female inebriate.

The pure cold water system is the republican system.

In 1844 the Central Division of the Sons of Temperance was also organized in Harrisburg by over 200 men (who must not have imagined their acronym—SOT), including Simon Cameron (whose cider jug was recently discovered in a clandestine cupboard at the Historical Society of Dauphin County). Their constitution was a model amalgam of common sense, morality, and good manners. They pledged themselves to practice temperance,

The first steam locomotive pulled the first passenger train into Harrisburg on September 16, 1839. The city soon became and long remained a major rail center. (HSDC)

Simon Cameron, a man of considerable wealth, acquired the Harris mansion from the heirs of John Harris, enlarged and Victorianized it, and dwelt there for the better part of half a century. He was perpetually active in the affairs of Harrisburg— including the temperance movement. In this, he showed a bit of harmless hypocrisy—his cider jug was recently found, hidden away behind a cupboard in his house. (HSDC) fellowship, and mutual aid, to avoid "ungenerous remarks and sarcastic language" at meetings, and to attend one another's funerals, "unless the brother died of some contagious or infectious disease." A man would not be admitted to the Sons if he were "incapacitated from earning a living" or if he received "five or more black balls" when the box was passed. If any brother took benefits by "feigning sickness," or if he "divulged the private affairs of the Order," or if he brought up for discussion a subject "of a sectarian or political character," or if he failed to purchase his own "regalia" when an officer, or if he broke his pledge not to "make, buy, sell, or use, as a beverage, any spiritous or malt liquors, wine, or cider," then he would be expelled from the brotherhood and his name "erased from the book." The boys spent most of their time preaching to the converted, in costume and comradeship.

Out in the countryside of Harrisburg, the temperance movement was more subtle, and possibly more effective. William Simonton's unpublished memoir *Notes on My Recollections of Country Life in West Hanover Township, Dauphin County, Pennsylvania* from the late 1830s shows how clever farmers scheduled sobriety without breaking up bottles and bars with an ax:

The custom of setting out the decanter and sugar bowl when friends made a social call, and of taking the bottle into the harvest field had been so long and generally in force, that working men claimed it as their right, no less than their privilege to have some stimulant "to keep them cool in summer, and warm and comfortable in winter!" Gradually however, by the substitution of "ginger small beer at 10 o'clock piece," and a dram of something

The farmers in this scene of haying (to say nothing of their mules) appear to be models of sobriety. It is nevertheless true that until the temperance movement achieved momentum in the 1830s and 1840s, the practice of lubricating the day's chores with alcohol was widespread. (HSDC)

Though it has been extensively altered, the John Elder house, built in 1740, is probably the oldest in Dauphin County. (HSDC)

stronger at regular meal time, the bottle was kept out of sight, and the opportunity for drinking to excess limited. In the course of a few years, the drinking usages thus curtailed were generally, though not wholly, abandoned, and the practice of having the decanter and glasses at hand on every social occasion, ceased to prevail among the more influential families. . .

If we have a little fun now reading the immensities of temperance reformers, we should be informed that public drunkenness and alcoholism were huge problems in the 19th century. Recent research shows that their fear and anger had substance and purpose. For example, in Spofford's *1843 Harrisburg Directory* we read that city brewers produced 465,000 gallons of beer and ale that year for 7,800 citizens. If just half of that amount was consumed in the city, and if half the city's population was male, and if half those males were between the ages of 20 and 70, and if half those adult males drank beer, then each of those 975 quaffed about two-thirds of a gallon of beer a day, accounting for five million bottles of beer in 1843.

Considering the immediate effects of Harrisburg's anti-slavery and temperance movements, it seems ironical that what the reformers boldly denounced, they did not immediately deter, and what they quietly detoured, they eventually got less of.

The Reverend Henry Boehm (1775-1877) linked 19th century Harrisburg to its colonial past. Until his death at the age of 102, he preached at the Locust Street Methodist Episcopal Church, which had grown from a log structure to an imposing masonry edifice. (HSDC)

The main building of the State Lunatic Hospital boasted this Lombardic tower. The atmosphere of the hospital was (and remains) more like that of an exclusive private school than that of an insane asylum. (HSDC) From Art Work of Harrisburg

V
SEVEN WOMEN HEALING

By the 1850s America was becoming a land of institutions, organizations, and associations. Alexis de Tocqueville had foreseen this development and wrote in the 1830s, "Americans of all ages, all conditions, and all dispositions constantly form associations.... The Americans make associations to give entertainments, to found seminaries, to build inns, to construct churches, to diffuse books, to send missionaries to the antipodes. In this manner they found hospitals, prisons, and schools."

One of the largest such institutions in Harrisburg was the State Lunatic Hospital. Founded in 1851, it was one of 38 state hospitals for the insane in existence by 1860. By 1901 another 100 had been built in the United States. Many of these institutions, including Harrisburg's, followed the ideal design which Dr. Thomas Kirkbride had first conceived in 1847, the same year the American Medical Association was formed and three years after the Association of Medical Superintendents of American Institutions for the Insane was established.

But if medicine was becoming well-organized by mid-century, it was still far from being well-practiced by modern standards. With all due respect, medical treatment in the past was nearly as much to be avoided as sickness itself. Anesthesia and antisepsis were undeveloped, and vaccination was not ubiquitous. Regular physicians, quacks, or homeopaths, they were quickly trained in a few months of coursework and apprenticeship. There was not very much to learn, in any case, so the black-coated, cane-carrying, horse-riding doctors were mainly admired for their character. They concocted their own medicines and tried to devise ways to make sure they were paid for their work. Dr. William Henry Egle, reflecting on the practice of medicine in Harrisburg, said, "Ah, me. I shudder when I think of it!"

The case records of patients at the Lunatic Hospital in Harrisburg show how "psychological medicine" was malpracticed there before the Civil War, and also how society in general thought about mind and body in those days.

February 25, 1858:

The most obvious but unknown institution in Harrisburg has always been the "state hospital," as we call it now. The Pennsylvania State Lunatic Hospital opened on October 6, 1851, under the management of 30-year-old Dr. John Curwen. It was located about a mile-and-a-half north of Harrisburg on 130 acres of farmland. It consisted of a central building with adjacent wings, so constructed that all would be "light and cheerful" with much "free natural ventilation" in keeping with the Victorian concern for "airy" surroundings. It had four floors, "a large Tuscan portico with a flight of twenty steps to the main entrance," a dome, and a view.

There were no accommodations at first for the "most violent and noisy class of patients" in the main building, so additional cottages were constructed for them on the grounds. These are the only original buildings still standing. The State Lunatic Hospital, in sum, looked like other asylums of its time—an architectural monument in a bucolic environment, both the building and the setting designed to relieve the mentally diseased.

The hospital stated its principles as inoffensively as possible in its *First Annual Report:*

There are those who believed, and many still continue to entertain the belief, that insanity is to be attributed to supernatural agency; that it is either a direct punishment from the Almighty, "by the visitation of God," for sins committed, or that it is through the agency of the Prince of Darkness.

That such might be the fact is not denied, but it is much more in accordance with true religion and sound philosophy to refer it to natural causes, which are known to be effective in its production. We know that the mind is influenced in different degrees by different and varying conditions of the bodily organization, even in health; and it is but one step farther, and a very natural one, in the chain of causes, to refer disordered manifestations of the

Looking more like the entrance to a country estate, the driveway to the Pennsylvania State Lunatic Hospital was meant to ease patients' entry into their new environment. (PHMC)

mind to diseased conditions of the bodily organs.

But if they thought insanity was certainly a medical problem, and probably not a religious one, the psychiatrists of the time ("alienists") believed it was nevertheless a moral problem, since insanity could influence one's "moral faculties." Thus, the hospital had to be morally as well as medically influential on its patients—it had a chapel, and the first gift donated was a "handsome Bible," arranged through the good offices of Miss Dorothea Dix, who had been influential herself in urging the state legislature to build the hospital. The staff was told to have "zeal" and "devotion," especially the assistant physician, who should visit all the patients every evening and "exert over them all the moral influence in his power." He would be assisted by the steward, who "shall observe the conduct of the inmates at the religious meetings." No drinkers would be hired, and there would be no smoking on the grounds. This ethos went by the official name of "moral treatment," meaning give the patients rest, recreation, sympathy, and morality. This treatment came at a price: the hospital would supplement its state appropriation by charging patients two dollars per week for room and board, if they were supported by the public, and three to 10 dollars per week, if they were private, depending on the "trouble" they were and their "ability to pay." ("Higher prices are paid by a special agreement with the superintendent for extra attention and accommodations.")

In 1858, 151 patients were admitted and 134 were discharged, either restored, improved, stationary, or dead, leaving 267 resident at the end of the year (119 were private patients, 148 public charges; 150

The pastoral setting of the Harrisburg State Hospital belies the often misguided, though well-intentioned, treatment once given to patients diagnosed as mentally ill. (PHMC)

were male, 117 female.) There was room for 300. The main disorders presented by the patients were acute and chronic "mania," "melancholy," and "dementia." There were also "imbeciles" and "epileptics." The causes of their disorders were undetermined in about half the cases, but otherwise 30 suspected causes were listed, including, at the top of the list, "domestic trouble" and "ill health." The most curious etiologies listed were "spiritual rappings," "female troubles," "politics," "religious excitement," "failure in business," "novel reading," "mortified pride," "exposure to the sun," and "excessive study."

Indeed, Dr. Curwen had more to say about the dangers of "excessive study" in the 1858 *Annual Report:*

The great tendency of the period is to over-exertion and stimulation in every department—the haste to be accounted learned, as well as the haste to be rich ... As a general thing children are sent to school too young ... they are encouraged and urged forward to a degree their powers are unable to bear ... under ten years of age very little mental effort should be required of children, and they should be allowed a large amount of exercise, bodily health and strength being more necessary and desirable than any learning at that age ... an incalculable amount of injury is done to those who have passed the age of ten ... youth of both sexes, between the age of ten and twenty, are expected to perform duties much beyond what should ever be required of them. . . .

Curwen was evidently wrong-headed in his worries. (Perhaps the young doctor's complaints were mainly disguising the troubles of his own scholastic, and mental, career—he entered Yale at 15.) Nearly all his male patients were farmers, laborers, merchants, craftsmen, and jobless men, and nearly all his female patients were the wives of such men. In eight years after the opening of the hospital, out of more than 1,000 patients treated, only 30 formally educated (and therefore possibly over-exercised) minds were admitted for a rest in this asylum.

In any case, those excerpts taken from the hospital's annual reports only hint at the nature of normal life in the institution—the features of its public face. We get a more intimate description of everyday reality by reading the superintendent's casebooks, especially the brief records of seven of the female patients who arrived in 1858.

Clara was admitted on February 25, 1858. She was single, age 20, and lived in Franklin County. Her attack was caused by "parental influence with an engagement." She would sit in a corner and cover her face with her hands. She was given "the usual purge" and pulverized

The laundry of the State Hospital was thoroughly modern. The women in uniform were undoubtedly members of the staff; but it is probable that the men, who are not in uniform, were patients assigned to work in the laundry as part of their therapy. Courtesy, Harrisburg State Hospital

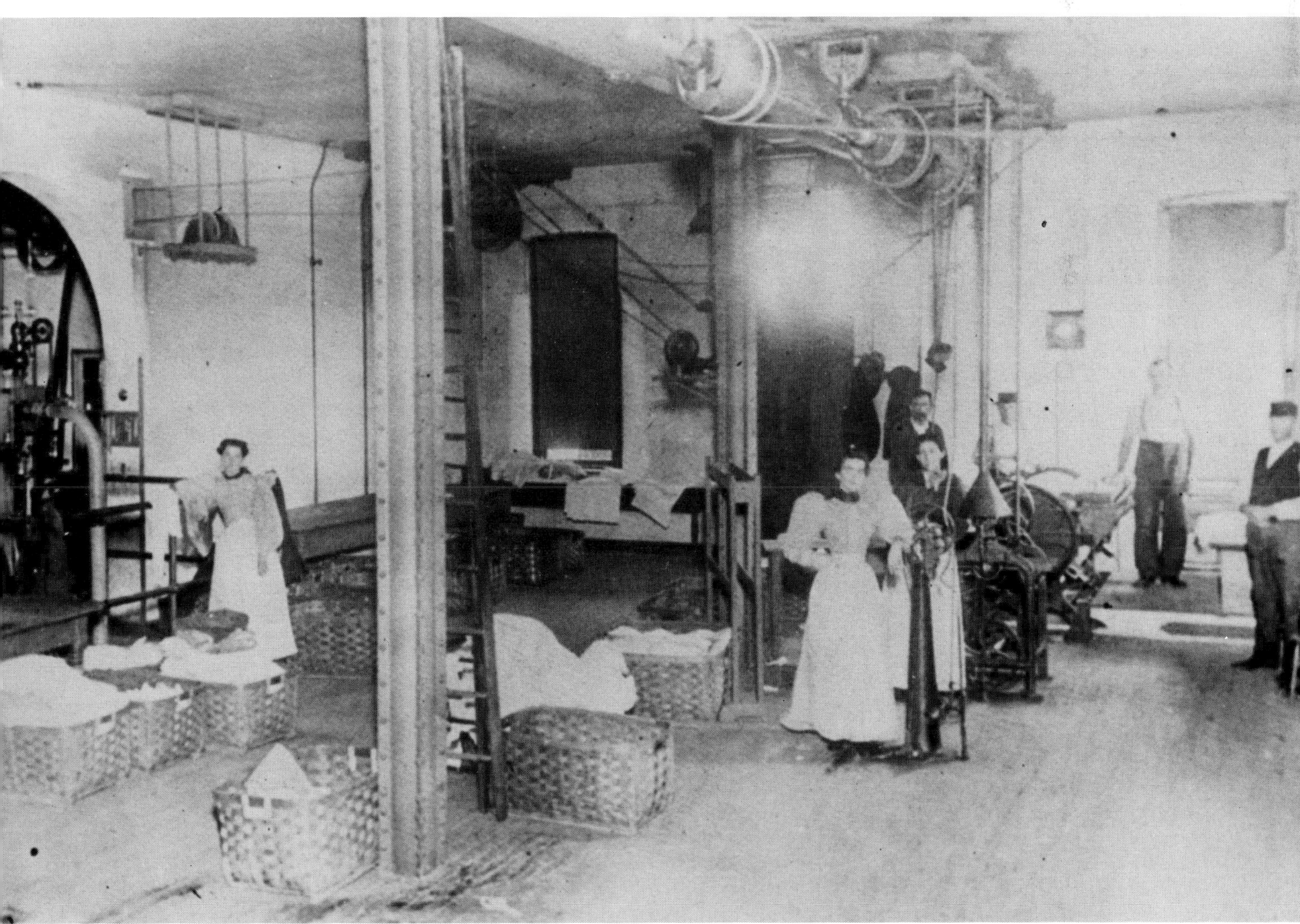

opium on admission. During her stay she was reported "careless in dress, often immodest." She was discharged after 6 months on August 21, 1858, her condition "improved."

Sarah was also admitted on February 25, 1858. She was born in Ireland and lived in Venango County. She was 33 and the wife of a store clerk. A week prior to admission she had received a "revelation of calamity for her friends and relatives," but also the assurance that "all will die happy." They purged her and administered liquid opium. They described her as "cheerful during good health, kind and benevolent, but has strong passions and deep prejudices." While riding in a carriage on the grounds she tried to escape. She was discharged after four months on June 20, 1858, her condition "without material change though at times improved and again becomes worse."

Leah was admitted on June 3, 1858. She was a "colored woman," age 40, and lived in Tioga. A week prior to admission she had become destructive. During 20 months preceeding confinement she had "lost seven children, which occasioned a great deal of anxiety." They purged her and gave her opium. They described her as "naturally kind and affectionate; though easily excited, is readily calmed." On June 20 she refused to wear clothing and was destructive. On September 2 a "fly plaster was put on her abdomen," and "after dressing with a poultice, granulated morphine was sprinkled on the surface." She died the same day.

Elizabeth was admitted on August 9, 1858. She was 41, the wife of a laborer, and lived in Schuykill County. Twelve days prior to admission she had become incoherent and evinced "a great fear of harmless objects and dogs; a slight interference with her plans would bring on an attack against others." She used tobacco, they noted. Her attack was caused, they said, by the death of her child 6 weeks ago and the loss of 4 others over a short time. She suffered from "hysterical and rheumatic affections; had forbodings of evil during all pregnancies." They let one quart of blood from her. She was purged and given opium. She was discharged after four months, on December 8, 1858, her condition "restored."

Jane was admitted on October 23, 1858. She was married, age 34, and lived in York County. A week prior to admission she had been incoherent and tore her clothes; this was caused by her "being threatened with divorce by her husband for some irregularities in her conduct." She was purged and given powdered opium. On February 14, 1859, about four months after admission, she died.

Catharine was admitted on November 18, 1858. She was married, age 45, and lived in Lebanon County. She had been "liable to hysterical troubles" since August, partly owing to the fact that even though she was a good church member, she "thinks she is lost forever by the idea that her profession of religion was that of a hypocrite." She was administered pulverized opium on admission, along with a purgative. When they interviewed her again in February 1859, they found that she was afraid to answer questions "for fear of error." In early June she said that

Opposite: *Treatment at the State Hospital emphasized light, air, activity, and medication. The presence of the female attendants tells us that this is the ladies' wing of the hospital. One can imagine Dr. Curwen's female patients recovering (or failing to recover) just beyond those open doors. Courtesy, Harrisburg State Hospital*

her children didn't belong to her and that she had no home. She was discharged and sent home on June 30, 1859, though she believed her husband now lived in the hospital and that she still had no home. Her condition after seven months was regarded as "improved."

Esther was admitted three days after Christmas in 1858. She was single, 21, and lived in Lancaster County. Two months prior to admission she began feeling that she was "good for nothing," because, she said, "her mother had neglected her upbringing," and thus, she was "different" from the other girls. The immediate reason for her admission, however, was her attempts to destroy herself by "holding her face under water and throwing herself off chairs." They purged her and gave her opium. She busied herself sewing and knitting. In early 1859 she made "abortive attempts now and then to hang herself," and "she spoke of starving herself." She was discharged after nine months on September 2, 1859, her condition "restored."

Notice the consistent qualities of these diagnoses. They suggest that women were perceived as being constitutionally unstable—they could be driven insane, supposedly, by body functions, interference in their love affairs, too religious devotion, the threat of divorce, the loss of children, and inattention by their own mothers. In effect, whenever a woman's fundamental feminine identity was disturbed (as Victorian culture defined both femininity and disturbance) it was guessed that she might go over the brink. And some of them probably did.

Notice the consistent, even monotonous, qualities of the therapies. They tried to keep the women busy, of course, but what is more revealing is the astonishing pharmacopia of chemicals administered. However important "moral treatment" was in antebellum asylums, these records show us that "medical" therapy was given to all patients. In fact, a tally of medication notes on all female patients' records in the 1850s shows that there were more than 90 different purgatives, emetics, sedatives, tonics, and other remedies the doctors could choose from. Most patients received four or five different medications on a sporadic schedule. These included "the usual purge," quinine, castor oil, ipecac, opium, morphine, calomel, powdered rhubarb, eggnog, and ice water injections (one suspects that patients improved in order that treatment might be stopped). All this was going on while the annual reports made it seem that recreation was the main activity—carriage rides, magic lantern shows, bowling, reading, and planting Simon Cameron's gift of vegetable seeds.

While she was doing research for me, Caroline Liebman found a tombstone on the grounds of the State Hospital. It marks the grave of Hannah Weber, age 34, who died there on September 26, 1866. Hannah was the only patient who left a "case record" in her own words:

Weep not my friends, why should I
[unclear] Or linger longer here
I now am freed from every woe
Relieved from every fear

She had finally found healing, despite everything the doctors could do for her.

Opposite: *Toward the end of the 19th century, many photographs of the State Hospital were taken, but they tend to concentrate far more on the facilities and the staff than upon the patients. No studies of female patients seem to have survived, but there is this picture of a dapperly dressed male patient and his dog. Courtesy, Harrisburg State Hospital*

Although Camp Curtin prepared men for bloody war, most of what occurred there was quite peaceable. For the care of the sick and wounded, the camp maintained a large, clean military hospital. (HSDC)

VI
THE LESSER BATTLES OF GREATER HARRISBURG

The Civil War was the most fundamental contest of American life. The North fought for the future—the necessity of nationhood, the first inklings of full equality, the whole might of industrial civilization organized against a moral and economic anachronism. The South fought for a "way of life"—the hard fact of slavery, a confederacy of agrarian communities, the dreams of manly and womanly honor.

Most of the war took place below the Mason-Dixon line, Pennsylvania's southern border—except one battle, when General Robert E. Lee brought 70,000 troops into the Commonwealth on the way to Harrisburg and Washington, D.C. He was intercepted by General George Meade and 93,000 men near Gettysburg, Pennsylvania on July 1, 1863. When they limped away from one another a few days later, more than 43,000 men were left behind on the ground, either killed or wounded. Meade was the "winner," inasmuch as Lee retreated. Union troops took Vicksburg, Mississippi, on July 4, and the Civil War began to end. Gettysburg was the greatest battle in the history of the Western Hemisphere (and one of America's most symbolic events), and Harrisburg was one of the largest targets that was never hit.

Here are some personal accounts from Camp Hill, the capital city, and Middletown about preparations for the invasion. They document the miss and its myth, as some Harrisburghers would claim more glory than the War Department would ever crown.

If wars are too important to be left to the generals, then perhaps they should be run by travel agents. They could look beyond the battle, and beyond the peace, to the eventual victory of trinket shops, highway markers, and historic inns. They would have told Custer, for example, to make his last stand within a short drive from Denver instead of Lodge Grass, Montana—in real estate and battlefield tourism, location is everything. Thus, if only a capital city tour guide had been at Cemetery Ridge to tell Meade to let Lee march a few miles farther in early July 1863, the Union still could have stopped the Rebels at the river and every child would have to memorize the Harrisburg Address and admire the stirring painting of "Pickett's Wade Across the Susquehanna." As it is, Gettysburg gets the glory.

Still, greater Harrisburg's preparations for war were important in its own history, and we are fortunate to have several private accounts of them. First, we have the brief narratives collected at the turn of the century by A.M. Bowman and submitted by Casper Dull to the Historical Society of Dauphin County in 1936. These give the view from the West Shore of the invasion. Dull's point was to prove that the Confederates got as far as Camp Hill just before the Battle of Gettysburg; to be specific, that they got to 32nd and Market streets, known then as Oyster's Point. Transcribed, typed, and bound like legal depositions, these testimonies from West Shore citizens remind us that it was great sport in those days to conjecture about what regiments marched how many yards in which direction, in preference to a discussion of what

the war, and the victory, were all about. The unexpected characteristics of these memoirs are the rancor they display against allies instead of the enemy and their Yankee drollery.

Mr. Martin Brinton testified that "We were between the Rebel pickets and the advance New York pickets. We were asked where we belonged.... One of our party said, 'We came out here to see how things looked.' The New Yorkers asked us if we saw any Rebels. Mr. Bates said, 'I had three or four for breakfast' ... the New York men had been taking fish, apple-butter, meat, blankets, bed clothing, etc. They had also taken old Mrs. Oyster's linen." Brinton then told of another coy conversation between Charles Flemming, a Union "spy" from Mechanicsburg, and some Confederate pickets. Flemming was sitting on a fence on the road between New Cumberland and White Hill. Several Rebels approached him on horseback and asked, "Have you seen any Rebels?" He said, "No Sir." They said, "Do we look like Rebels?" He said, "I don't know, you are all strangers to me."

Mr. Z. Bowman also thought ill of the New York troops stationed on the West Shore. He swore that "New Yorkers turned out to be our worst enemies. They killed our hogs, chickens, and so on." He saw them wearing the "great high hats" they'd stolen from Mrs. Oyster. "Nice mark to shoot at," he said.

Mr. Samuel Shopp repeated many of the previous themes in his testimony. He swore that "The raid was in July. I forget just what year." On the matter of bombardment, he said, "I guess I picked up about fifteen shells that were not exploded,

and I gave them nearly all to parties who wanted them as relics—some in Philadelphia, New York City, and other places." On the matter of Rebels and New Yorkers: "I only talked to a few of the Rebels. They were not very sociable. I heard one of them say they 'got into Pennsylvania, but they didn't know how the devil to get out."

John Mater mentioned a close call he had with a mysterious stranger:

He wore black clothes, a splendid black frock coat, and was about five feet ten inches in height, and slightly built. A

Fort Washington was built in 1863 when the Union feared the Confederate army would not be stopped at Gettysburg. The earthworks were still visible, though overgrown, by the time of this 1930 photo. (HSDC)

Opposite: *General Joseph F. Knipe, a native of Harrisburg, was in charge of the city's defenses when Lee's army invaded Pennsylvania. At some point in the hostilities, he paused long enough to sit in full battle dress for an unknown photographer. (HSDC)*

fine looking man. He had a straight knife on his belt . . . It hung below his coat two or three inches. I asked him if he was going out to our fellows. He said, "No, the dumb devils would just as soon shoot their friends as their enemies. . . ." He was a spy. We knew he was a Rebel. . . .

Mater closed with the speculation that "The Rebels could have easily gone into Harrisburg, if it wasn't for the Battle of Gettysburg. We had a bad set of men—those New Yorkers."

The view from Harrisburg of the invasion is presented in a full narrative by Henry Demming. This was written at Casper Dull's request in 1900. Demming was in a good position to be a thorough observer; though less than 21, he had already served three enlistments in the Union army by July 1863, and while

recuperating in Harrisburg from two wounds he was the City Editor of the *Daily Telegraph*. He began,

Refugees began coming in considerable numbers as early as the 20th of June, and sometimes the old Harrisburg bridge was choked up with farmers and others fleeing from a threatening foe. There was a constant flow through Harrisburg, from west to east, of all sorts of vehicles, as well as droves of cattle, horses, sheep and swine. The people of Harrisburg who remained in the city wondered where all the fleeing people came from, as the flow was so continuous and large.

The first sound of war that Harrisburg heard was on Tuesday evening, June 30, when Confederate forces were met in Camp Hill by General Joseph Knipe's troops. After this engagment, units were raised to

defend the city. They dug in by Harris' grave. They had reason to anticipate the worst, since everyone had seen the glare given by the burning of the Columbia bridge and the Carlisle barracks on the night of June 28.

But the only assault they stopped was a spy's mission about four o'clock in the morning of July 2. First Corporal Demming himself caught the man, who was dressed as a cavalry captain and hiding on a raft in the river. He was locked up for a while, but for some reason was released, then captured again. This would seem to be a fairly mundane encounter, but Demming made a good deal of it in his memoir. First, he quoted from a story he had written for the *Telegraph* on July 2:

. . . a flat boat was discovered coming down stream, containing what was supposed to be a man. The guard ordered the person who was on board to stop the craft, but the order not being obeyed he fired. This had the effect of causing the occupant of the boat (which, by the way, had just struck a rock and remained fast), to dodge down and secrete himself in the inside. He was warned to get up and run his boat in to the shore where the guard was, but not complying a second shot was fired at the boat. This had no effect, and the corporal of the guard, accompanied by Sergeant Gratz, of the same company, took possession of another boat, lying along the shore, and pulled out to the flat. On nearing it, it presented a deserted appearance; but when the craft came alongside, lo, and behold, a man with the uniform of a cavalry officer, and wearing a captain's straps, was discovered cramped up in one corner of the flat boat.

He was arrested and ordered to leave the flat and get into the boat alongside.

This he did, but not without remonstrating sometime with his captors, protesting against being arrested in this ungentlemanly manner, as he termed it, and rudely compelled by subalterns to leave his own boat. When the party reached the shore, the officer was searched and a loaded four shooter (Sharp's), and a new hatchet taken from him.

When they took the uniform off the man, who gave his name as J.H.M. Weitbrecht, they found a map of the Susquehanna on which fords had been marked.

The capstone of Demming's memoir to Dull was this testimony:

Fully twenty years after the close of the Rebellion a former captain of General Stuart's Black Horse cavalry called to see me at Harrisburg, and stated that if the Confederate captain had not been captured at Harris Park the night of July 1-2, 1863, that a portion of Stuart's command would have crossed the Susquehanna at the ford opposite Camp Curtin that morning, burned all the public buildings, levied from the citizens $500,000 in cash, besides provisions, and carried off a number of the most prominent residents as hostages. He also stated that the supposed Rebel captain was an officer of another rank, the "dare devil" of the Confederate army; that when captured he gave an assumed name, and had a number of confederates in Harrisburg at the time; that he escaped from Fort Delaware, rejoined the Confederate army. . . .

Demming did nothing to temper the hyperbole in his memoir to Casper Dull. On the very first of the 14 pages, he wrote:

Several Confederate officers told me

afterwards that their belief was if the capital city of the second state of the Union could be captured, the capital lying so far north of Washington, they would be recognized as a confederacy, or at least as belligerents, by the nations of Europe; that this would lead to the opening of the ports of the South; and, with the ports not blockaded, they could secure all the munitions of war desired, and ultimately their independence.

If Harrisburg could not boast about a battle, at least it could be proud to imagine what it had prevented (nothing less than the collapse of Western civilization, apparently), for if Henry Demming, able catcher of spies, had not done his duty, one could guess that the South might have won the war and left the house divided.

Of course, Demming was not lying—he was only inflating, as did other memorialists of the Civil War, many of them finding warrant for saying that they and their comrades had been the proverbial blacksmiths who had kept the nail from falling out of the horse's shoe, thus saving the shoe, the horse, the rider, the message, the battle, the war, and the nation.

Lastly, we read the view of the invasion seen from the interior of the East Shore, available in the diary of R.I. Young of Middletown. Young first tried to get into the war on Wednesday, June 24, when he went to Harrisburg. The next day he tried "to get Eby to go in a cavelry with me but he would not go so I came home at half past one." He had his chance in Middletown by Saturday the 27th: "In the evening their was a meeting in the square for the purpos of starting a company." Young and his comrades were formally

organized the next day: "At nine oclock we had a meeting and all that signed their names to the company fell in rank and Rover marched us around town and then we adjourned to meet at seven in the evening." They hadn't been able to convince everyone in town, however, that the danger was sufficient: "Some others would not go becaus they would not go out of town," he wrote.

But with the help of his father ("Father told me he would take me to Harrisburg if I would go over the river in the trenches"), Young got up a crowd and went to Camp Curtin. They drew rations for 18 men and then went into the city to draw arms, but the armory was closed.

The next day, June 29, they started back to Middletown with 240 guns and 9,000 rounds of ammunition. "We got home about seven and some of the boys had a fite," he wrote, but Young and a friend were able to organize another company of 40 men in less than three hours. Eight of them, including the diarist, guarded a ford until four in the morning.

The next day, June 30, they mustered the new company and

Copied from a daguerreotype, circa 1860, this photograph of a horse and carriage is considered the oldest surviving photographic image of Harrisburg. (HSDC)

FIRST NATIONAL BANK
ORGANIZED JANUARY 1, 1864
PRESIDENT
John H. Briggs
STOCKHOLDERS
Simon Cameron
William Colder
James Young
Geo. T. Hummel
David Fleming
George H. Small
Rud. F. Kelker
CASHIER
George H. Small
STOCKHOLDERS
J. D. Cameron
Jacob R. Eby
Thomas A. Scott
Wm. T. Hildrup
John Brady
John H. Briggs
T. D. Greenawalt
FIRST NATIONAL BANK
JAMES BRADY   G. M. McCAULEY
TELLER   GEO. W. SMALL
CLERKS
N. E. COR. SECOND & WALNUT ST.
HARRISBURG, PA.
Executed with a Steel Pen by A. F. Small. April, 1865.

elected officers. Young became 3rd Sergeant. They drilled again in the evening, and went on picket again all night. And they drilled again the next day—if the Rebels invaded, Middletown's defenders would be orderly.

Late at night on July 3, there was a commotion:

The foundry bell rang and all the companies came out for it was an alarm but when they looked to see who rang the bell they could not be found so D. Cambell went in the shop and up in the garret we fount two of the boys and two down stairs we took them to the [squire's] office and he charged them two dollars a peace.

That was as much alarm as Middletown would have to bear. On the 4th of July Young's company "marched all over town" again. It was time for Young's father to spur him again: "father told me he would equip me if I would go so I went to Harrisburg." In the city he per-suaded Donald Cameron (Simon Cameron's son) "to go to the captin and see if he would take me." Young was not able to find out until Sunday if a company would take him. In any case, he never informed his diary; on Sunday, July 5, he only wrote "I was in Harrisburg all day." That was his last entry. Did he become a soldier, abandon his civilian diary, and start a war journal? There is no record of any R.I. Young becoming a member of a Pennsylvania unit during the Civil War. Perhaps he simply retired his diary and went back to Middletown when he saw that there would be no invasion.

These Civil War narratives from Camp Hill, Harrisburg, and Middletown are not quite as momentous as the chronicles of Gettysburg or even Carlisle, which was actually shelled and occupied. But the plain quality of Greater Harrisburg's days of war is worth knowing, for it shows the ennui that was the enemy of most men most of the time.

Opposite: *Harrisburg's early banking community was made up of its most prominent citizens. While many of the individuals listed on this poster are not familiar to most present-day Harrisburghers, their names can be found on many local streets. (HSDC)*

Despite the city's preparations (and perhaps some keen anticipation in certain quarters) Harrisburg sat untouched as the Civil War passed it by. Nearby Carlisle, as shown in Thomas Nast's drawing, was shelled by rebel troops and subsequently occupied. Courtesy, Cumberland County Historical Society

"Pappy" Boyer was a leader of the drive to clean up the Eighth Ward, considered to be Harrisburg's moral low spot. When he was not busy with such crusades or with his job as Poor Director, Boyer entertained the youngsters of Harrisburg with, first, this "kiddy tram," and, later, an automobile. (HSDC)

VII
THE FUNERAL OF HARRY COOK IN THE OLD "ATE" WARD

By 1877 the Reconstruction of the South was over. Northern troops had been withdrawn from the conquered province, and both sides were free to concentrate on the material matters at hand—the completion of the industrial revolution. Rutherford B. Hayes, having just been elected President even though 250,000 more citizens had voted for Samuel J. Tilden, started Easter egg hunts on the Capitol lawn. Party politics and public architecture both became Byzantine in their complexity. In Pennsylvania, Senator Simon Cameron directed the former while the brilliant Frank Furness designed the latter. Also in Pennsylvania, according to Otto Bettman, "The railroad companies drew the map of the urban age. Altoona was a child of the Pennsylvania. The Lackawanna turned Slocum's Hole into Scranton." The railroads drew their way right into town—in Philadelphia the tracks came to the doorsteps of City Hall, the biggest building in America before the Pentagon. In Harrisburg the tracks cut the city in half, from top to bottom, but John Harris' and William Maclay's early planning had denied them the riverfront. There was a Grand Opera House built at Third and Walnut, and a high obelisk erected at Second and State to honor Civil War soldiers. Horses instead of men were now pulling the fire trucks around the city from blaze to blaze.

Mark Twain and Charles Dudley Warner would name a novel after these years—The Gilded Age, a time when the surface of life was shiny and expensive, hiding whatever base metal was beneath it. By watching the funeral of Harry Cook in Harrisburg, one can scratch this city's bright surface and see the rowdy life below it.

April 29, 1877:

One day in 1912, as the demolition began in the Eighth Ward just east of the Capitol, an anonymous historian, looking at the leveling from one of the Capitol's windows, spoke his remembrance of the locale. We are drawn to it especially for his account of the funeral of Morris Henry Cook, who, with his wife Hattie, had owned the Ward's Lafayette Hall, famous in the past as a gambling den and rum mill.

I'll never forget the funeral of Harry Cook. [When] he died his wife determined that he should have a gorgeous funeral, with brass band accompaniment. Fancy that. On the day of the funeral the remains lay in state in the barroom, surrounded by floral tributes galore from the loving wife. Deceased was attired in his best suit, lavender trousers, black velvet coat, with rose in the lapel, low cut vest, open front starched shirt containing a diamond pin as big as the end of your thumb, low collar with wide-flowing white scarf, side-whiskers and moustache waxed to needle points. And that casket was solid rosewood with a plethora of silver ornaments and a large silver plate containing name, age and date of death of deceased. From early morn to the time set for the funeral, there was a constant stream of people going and coming to look upon the face of Harry. And the funeral procession was one never to be forgotten. First came the brass band playing the Dead March, followed by the minister and pallbearers, and then the hearse decorated with floral emblems. Then came the widow in deep mourning in a carriage all by herself, followed by at least fifty carriages containing the dead man's intimates and denizens of the underworld. Before the casket was closed the big diamond stud was taken from the dead man's shirt front, and his diamond rings, three in number, removed from his fingers. Hundreds followed the procession, and altogether it was such a funeral as is described by Mark Twain in telling of the burial of Buck Fanshaw. So, too, events in the Eighth ward were dated from Harry Cook's funeral.

The event has remarkable lessons to teach us about everyday life in the old "Ate" Ward. Like the funerals of Chicago mobsters in the 1920s, the last rites of Harry Cook reveal something of the relationship between underworld and overworld.

The popularity and panache of the funeral suggest that the saloon keeper had countless customers wanting every kind of miscreant's recreation, and so often that Harry and Hattie became a singularly wealthy partnership. But their prosperity was probably not able to purchase them official respectability, so they took advantage of the right occasion both to copy and to mock the propriety of those who had gotten rich correctly.

Suit Harry like a Sultan, follow him like a Pharaoh, inter him like the Inca. Buy the blessing of the priest and the bonhomie of the police. Choose the choicest coffin for the corpse, afford the finest fragrance from the florist. Gather a group that nears the size of the lamenting for Lincoln. And afterwards with every bottle and bet, the Eighth will elevate him more than all the mayors.

Harry Cook, "tall, well-proportioned, handsome, of commanding appearance, a ready and effective conversationalist," was dead at 40. He was, according to his remembrancer, the Eighth Ward's most "typical and representative"

This cigar store Indian has a long history of ownership in Dauphin County. It is now in the collection of the Historical Society of Dauphin County. Photo, Mark H. Dorfman

citizen. His constituents included many recently emigrated Russian Jews and even more blacks, who had been ensconced in the Eighth Ward long before (some were escapees from slavery). They lined the streets at his funeral, and "many a dusky eye shed tears," for Cook was said to have had "a heart readily touched by tales of woe. He had given money lavishly to the poor and the needy. He had helped bury the dead of these poor folk when men who would have considered Harry Cook's touch contamination had turned coldly away."

But if Harry was "typical," his Lafayette Hall was hardly common. It was described as being like "certain pretentious resorts of the day in New York." The basement was a restaurant, the first floor an ornate barroom, and the next floor "a free-and-easy dance hall where most anything would go." Even the Hall's

Although the tobacco shop at the left can scarcely be taken as a sign of depravity, this is an aspect of the Eighth Ward by day. This view of West Alley from North Street shows a neighborhood going to seed and eventually to be obliterated. (HSDC)

Harrisburg's letter carriers sat for this group portrait in 1879. The city's first letter carrier, Jonas K. Rudy, is in the middle of the front row. President James K. Polk appointed Rudy in 1847. (HSDC)

stalls for horses had mirrors. The Lafayette was connected to other buildings in the neighborhood that were managed by Hattie Cook.

The low life collecting in Lafayette Hall had three sources. First, there were the canal boat men ("the men who followed the tow path . . . were not generally the men who sought out a prayer meeting when they tied up for the night"). Then there were the Up-River Yankees ("For months they wrought laboriously amidst primeval solitudes . . . with the Spring freshets, they would take their rafts to the lower Susquehanna . . . many of them made Harrisburg their objective point for a seance with the various phases of sin prior to their departure for another long era of cutting and logging"). And finally there were the Civil War Yankees—about 300,000 en toto lolled around Camp Curtin in the northern part of Harrisburg during the 1860s.

The soldiers at Camp Curtin had "money to burn and a burning desire to spend it," and in Harrisburg there were "maids of the town, and matrons too, whose husbands were at the front, who were willing to assist in the depletion of plethoric pocketbooks." The camp's "wild young blades, freed from the shackles of home restraint," rushed to the Eighth Ward, where, on Sundays especially, the "drink flowed in maddening swirls," and "brutal fights commenced." For many years thereafter, wrote one reporter, the city was jammed with "flotsam and jetsam, storm-tossed wreckage on life's sea, that dated from Camp Curtin days."

After the Civil War there was a fourth source of low life in the Eighth Ward, the State Street Bridge Gang. In 1873 a bridge was completed on State Street over the Pennsylvania Railroad tracks. It protected pedestrians from one danger but exposed them to another as the bridge became a hangout for the Eighth Ward "toughs," who were reputed to be even rougher than the "Sixteen Bleeders." They bullied and robbed citizens bottlenecked at the bridge until an even tougher judge put one of them in jail for two years for stealing a dime.

All the while the Eighth was rugged, some efforts were made to damp the debauch. In the 1870s a moral crusade was begun by businessmen, the evangelist Samuel Sayford, and Poor Director Charles

The second Rockville Bridge replaced its wooden predecessor in 1877. The famed stone arch bridge would in turn replace this steel structure crossing the Susquehanna River and the Pennsylvania Canal. (HSDC)

Dauphin County Court judges John Snyder, John Pearson, and Isaac Mumma posed in the courtroom in front of a trompe l'oeil painting of Justice for this 1870s photo. (HSDC)

The beaux arts-style Harrisburg Post Office is shown under construction in 1880. A building with a distinguished air, it was razed in the 1960s to make way for the black cube Federal Building. (HSDC)

Boyer. They got Harry Cook's liquor license rescinded, and Harrisburg's "last glorious palace of sin" was emptied after Cook's death. About 20 years later, John W. Brown turned the Hall into a Rescue Mission. He left the decor more or less the same: the marble bar stayed, and behind it all the cobwebbed bottles, "but the walls that once re-echoed to bald blasphemy and obscene jests were now the scene of earnest prayer and melodious songs of praise."

The rest of the Eighth Ward was born again in 1912, when the plans for the Capitol Park Extension were completed. Demolition was vigorous until 1919, then measured until the project was finished in 1940. Now Harry Cook's old neighborhood is lawn and state office buildings. Between Walnut and North streets and Fourth Street and the Pennsylvania Railroad tracks, the wreckers removed 527 buildings, including hundreds of residences, a brewery, market house, shoe company, coach works, iron foundry, several hotels, fire houses, churches, and schools.

The *Harrisburg Telegraph* seemed a little sad about the wrecking as it began in 1912, but covered it mainly as "progress" since the old Ward had been the city's biggest pen for black sheep—"crimes beyond number have been committed in the Eighth Ward . . . some of the most sensational murders on the police records of the city have had the Eighth Ward for a stage setting." Also in 1912, J. Howard Wert, a moralist who seemed delighted to write about immorality, began publishing a series of three dozen articles on "The Passing of the Old Eighth"; these essays, quoted often here, remain our best sources on its everyday history.

The Eighth was a classic example of the fleshpots that existed around industrial entrepots in late Victorian America. The Ward was allegedly notorious around the state, but it could not have been much worse in its time than Philadelphia's and Pittsburgh's worst neighborhoods. But it was probably more decadent, in its own way, than anything we would dream to demolish in Harrisburg in our time. If you believe in clean, uncrowded streets, legal products and merchants, and fairly gentle nights—all civilized virtues, certainly—then you will likely view the evacuation and pacification of the Eighth Ward as a "reform." Yet, it is clear that the Ward served certain human needs, for how could it have prospered otherwise? It was the scene for the expression of particular types of manhood and womanhood, and the only "community" many deviates and minorities could find.

The Eighth Ward in its heyday and Harry Cook both seem to have passed into history undocumented by any surviving photographs. The pictures that do survive give only a hint of the rough-and-tumble life of the streets. Here is the West Side of Filbert Street looking north from Walnut in 1910. (HSDC)

The Bolton Hotel, now known as the Warner, has been a landmark on Market Square since the mid-19th century. In this early 20th-century postcard, the Bolton proudly displays a mansardic roof that was probably added in the 1870s. (PHMC)

*The members of the Harrisburg Wheel Club proudly display
their "ordinaries," the high-wheeled bicycles that added
adventure to the new sport. (HSDC)*

VIII
CHILDREN'S DAY AT
THE DAUPHIN
COUNTY CENTENNIAL
CELEBRATION

The late 19th century was a time for celebrations in America. There were hundreds of hundredth birthday parties in towns, counties, states, and the nation itself. The Centennial Exposition in Philadelphia in 1876 saluted the signing of the Declaration of Independence. The party was set up in Fairmount Park inside 180 buildings, including the largest wooden building ever nailed together in America. President Grant and Emperor Dom Pedro of Brazil turned on a giant steam engine that powered the whole affair.

Other similarly symbolic and national displays abounded. Yellowstone National Park had opened in 1872, a tribute to nature. The National Baseball League was organized in 1876, saluting sport (the first All-American football team would be announced in 1889). The first national Labor Day was held in New York in 1882, a recognition of human energy. Buffalo Bill Cody brought out his national Wild West Show in 1883, a paean to the frontier past. The Brooklyn Bridge, symbol of greatest engineering, was completed in 1883, and the Washington Monument, shrine to the greatest patriot, was capstoned in 1884. The Statue of Liberty, come-on to the world, was done in 1886.

Dauphin County's Centennial Celebration of 1885 was the local example of this national spirit that hoped to bring the country together, toast it, and then move it forward. The details of Children's Day on September 14, however, suggest the house was still divided against itself.

September 14, 1885:

Harrisburg's Centennial was sensational. The celebration lasted four days, from Monday, September 14, 1885, to Thursday the 17th, and brought 100,000 people into town. The first day was Children's Day, the second, Military and Civic Day, the third, Industrial Display Day, and the fourth, Firemen's Day.

An antiquarian display ran throughout the celebration, and it was the city's biggest flea market ever. Though no antiques were sold, only shown, it included anything imaginably historical, from the founder John Harris' silver knee buckles to a wooden cup made from the tree to which his father was tied; from Captain Eli Daugherty's embattled pocket Bible and gold watch ("A Confederate bullet struck the watch . . . and then penetrated the Bible, stopping about half way") to W. Wallace Geety's leftover grapeshot ("entered Mr. Geety's head at the base of the nose"); from D.S. Early's wooden cuckoo clock ("Very old") to John B. Cox's blunderbuss ("No history"). It sounds just like the sort of artifactual sideshow the old Historical Society of Dauphin County would have sponsored. It was "conceded on all sides the most unique, as it was the most successful, exhibition of the kind ever held in this or any other country."

The volume documenting the celebration, *Centenary Memorial of the Erection of the County of Dauphin and the Founding of the City of Harrisburg* was edited by the famous local historian Dr. William Henry Egle and published a year later. Setting aside the pieces of the true mulberry tree, *Centennial* is probably the city's most ubiquitous memorabilia; boxes of them can still be bought. Like so many salutes from the past, it is full of lists of committees, names, numbers, things, and all the words of all the speeches their leaders gave.

Between the lines of all this propriety, and oftentimes right in them, we can find unofficial insights into Harrisburg's social life a hundred years ago. This is especially the case with Finley Thomas' recounting of the details of the parade on Children's Day; he was an eyewitness because he was the Chief Marshal.

Harrisburg, wrote Thomas, brought in the first day of the Centennial celebration with "whoop and hurrah, and ding dong, and boom and whizz." A cannon shot started it all, then church bells chimed. Trains and wagons came in full of "country cousins" from everywhere, "all bent on having a good time." The city was festooned with flags, bunting, and gaudy calico, "But like Harrisburg, it never awakened to the fact that it *ought to decorate* until the last hour . . . It

Dr. William Henry Egle (1831-1901), when not engaged in the practice of medicine, became the principal historian of Harrisburg and Dauphin County in the 19th century. This daguerreotype shows him in his early twenties, obviously keen to begin his twofold career. (HSDC)

This late 19th century postcard celebrates one of Harrisburg's firehouses and its up-to-date equipment. (PHMC)

The Rockville Bridge, north of Harrisburg, is justly acclaimed as the longest stone arch bridge in the world. (PHMC)

seemed as if they realized for the first time that Harrisburg was really going to have a Centennial celebration to amount to something."

"The school children took possession of Harrisburg on Monday," he continued. They collected in their classrooms around town by 8:15 that morning, ready for the invasion of Harris Park, along the river. Perhaps with forethought of the chaos to come, "many teachers absented themselves and refused to take part in the proceedings."

Thomas thought he saw ethnic groups mingled. The children "were of all sorts, sizes, and conditions and colors. There were children of all nationalities—from the fresh-looking, sturdy thoroughbred American through the gamut of English, French, Swede, Irish, Italian, German and every other country." He also thought he saw classes mingled. "The boy whose father can count his money by the thousands marched linked arms with the lad whose father works for ninety cents

The Harris Park School as it appeared around 1890 gives an idea of the solid structures the city was providing for the education of its children. Here the 4,542 youngsters assembled to march to John Harris's nearby grave. (HSDC) From Art Work of Harrisburg

a day as a laborer." Those two classes were at truce together on account of their similar sentiment for their country's sign: "They both wore the American flag on their bosoms." He thought that sign even allowed the races to mingle: "The little colored boy bore aloft his flag and marched with the same saucy, independent step as his whiter school-fellow." But the schools were segregated, and so was the march. According to the text, the children would proceed in the following order:

Verbeke street school, estimated 525 children in charge of supervisory principal and teacher.
Lincoln school (colored), North Street, W. H. Layton, principal, 60 scholars.

Calder street school (colored) marshaled by Mr. Scott, 50 scholars.
Paxtang school, Miss Kate Miller, principal, 70 scholars.

When there was drill order, Thomas credits that to the difference between boys and girls. "The girls, as a rule, marched better than the boys, although the Harris Park boys made a pretty appearance sixteen abreast."

While the children rendezvoused at Harris Park around the grave of John Harris the elder, "a livelier crowd was never seen." The girls, again, were generally "quiet and well-behaved," but the "true boys," again, "held high carnival." Possibly forgetting the code of concord, they took time for a "few fights":

Links with the past are seen in the above faces of two female centenarians, and a dignified legislative doorkeeper, all recorded in late 19th-century photographs. (HSDC)

Dr. Eysler looks on while young pharmacist Harry O. Millen compounds a prescription in Eysler's Drug Store, circa 1885. (HSDC)

A newspaper reporter separated two boys who were at it hammer and tongs to the great delight of their school-fellows. Two boys banged each other over the head with flag sticks, and were parted; but it was all in fun, and so then and there over the grounds the lads had little battles, which lasted a few minutes, and then the participants were good friends again.

When they arrived at the obelisk at Second and State streets, the children sang "My Country 'Tis of Thee," and prepared to be issued their souvenir, a card about seven by nine inches depicting an earlier tribe of spirited Americans sportive in their own way (a picture of "An Attempt to Burn John Harris at the Present Site of Harrisburg, in the

Year 1720"). Each youth was to receive a card after countermarching by the monument. Scanning the 4,542 pairs of hands (the official count, at least), the organizing committee "determined to carry out the programme and the band was ordered to play. It did so with a will and the countermarch began." Each child got his momento, if "amid much shouting and jostling."

Later that evening the Court House was filled with an "intelligent" audience ready for an "intellectual treat," a speech by Judge John Bayard McPherson. Besides the cerebral sort in the crowd, "also many ladies graced the occasion with their smiling, beauteous and benign presence."

General Simon Cameron, the Centennial's organizer, introduced their orator. The Judge had much to insist. Harrisburg's history was the struggle of free men against nature and savage, he said, until "man touched the shoulder of his fellow-man and set himself to establish social order." They had done that today, he claimed:

Our race knows well the power of an ordered state, yields easily to wise restraint, will bear, nay, will command, that rule be strong on fit occasion; . . . through every form it does demand the substance of control. In the main this principle has not been shaken, and today it is the base on which our massive strength finds rest.

Jos. Claster's clothing and notion store was housed in an old building at the southeast corner of Second and Chestnut streets. The unpaved streets and the trolley tracks were typical of 1890s Harrisburg. (HSDC)

Although the centennial celebration of 1885 was an extravagant civic wingding, few photographs survive to memorialize it. A great welcoming arch was built at the corner of Fifth and Market streets. It is pictured here just as the celebration was getting underway. (HSDC)

But the control and the order of that celebration day were only skin deep even when they showed. Thomas' observations inadvertently reveal a society quite taken with differences between native and immigrant, rich and poor, black and white, young and old, and male and female. He had witnessed disunity, but interpreted it as unity.

In his prayer before noon at the Court House, after the parade, the Reverend William Harris read the morning's general events more deeply and worriedly than either Judge McPherson or Chief Marshal Thomas:

Defend our liberties, preserve our unity, save us from violence, discord and confusion, from pride and arrogancy, and from every evil way. Fashion into one happy people the multitude brought hither out of many kindred and tongues.

The Old Home Week parade of 1905 included these women's groups. (HSDC)

IX
HARRISBRAG

By the time Americans saw the 20th century arriving, they also noticed the trouble the 19th century had left behind. Forty years of remarkable urban and industrial growth needed to be reconsidered, redirected, and reorganized—reformed, in short. This was the time for "progressivism" of one sort or another in government and society. Its leaders were Presidents Theodore Roosevelt and Woodrow Wilson, Governors John Altgeld, Robert M. LaFollette, and Hiram Johnson, and countless mayors, professionals, journalists, and businessmen. Their national achievements included passage of such laws as the Sherman Anti-Trust Act (1890), the Pure Food and Drug Act (1906), and the Federal Trade Commission Act (1914). At the state and municipal levels, the initiative, referendum, recall, direct primary, and short ballot reforms were most significant.

Progressivism had its aesthetic side too, which can be seen in the "City Beautiful" movements of the early 20th century. The idea was to up-date urban life, especially by building modern transportation, sanitation, and recreation systems, and even more noticeably by landscaping great parks. The supreme achievement was Frederick Law Olmsted's Central Park in New York City. The broad plazas, green spaces, and ornate monuments of the Chicago World's Fair of 1893 were also models for other cities to follow. All this required careful coordination by public and private leaders.

Harrisburg's beautification and modernization, which is still appreciated, was among the best-planned and best-looking projects in the country. We begin this story by looking at a little public relations pamphlet published by the Harrisburg Daily Telegraph *in 1904, puffery to the city's progress supposedly written by its carrier boys.*

If you are looking for highfalutin' phrases, neatly turned sentences and Websterian ponderosity, understand right now that you will not find them here. This is going to be a plain statement of fact and facts . . . We believe in Harrisburg. . . .

The *Telegraph* carrier boys' pitch to the city might be admired for its vigor, if not its artfulness. Their 20-page New Year's card for 1904 tried to list everything the city should be famous for. "Proud? You bet," they said. "Harrisburg has outgrown the clothes of ten years ago and is beginning to put on a brand new suit of the latest style, made by experts." They wanted their readers to know that the city would take "the biggest brace in its history this year," that "the whole country" had begun "to talk of the Harrisburg idea," including "thousands of newspapers." This place, they said, "is not a bump on a log. She moves and keeps a-movin'."

In 1904 "almost all" the greater Harrisburg area's citizens "come to town to shop," they claimed, and those shoppers would soon have more paved streets to travel on. The water filtration plant on Island Park would soon be completed. "Harrisburg does not live in the dark at night"—there were 450 street lights. They counted 180 "schools" in the city! A new Masonic temple was being built, a new city hall was promised, the new state capitol would be finished by next January, and a new Reading passenger station was scheduled to open in April. "There may be some vacant houses in Harrisburg," they said, but only "for a minute," because there were

The proposed view of the new capitol closely resembles the project as completed. The elaborate statuary over the portico, however, was never finished. The plaza in front of the capitol is used for a legislative parking lot today. (HSDC)

22 building and loan associations scurrying to satisfy buyers and sellers. There were three telegraph and two telephone companies, 19 daily and weekly newspapers, and 100 passenger trains landing each day. "In this respect . . . Harrisburg is several to the good over Philadelphia." The city boasted "the finest Young Men's Christian Association building in the state, outside of Philadelphia," a "magnificent amusement hall—the Lyceum," a new steel bridge over the river, the state champion baseball team, and "the best" athletic grounds.

What did the city manufacture? Four thousand men worked in city iron and steel factories and 8,000 "on our borders" (meaning Steelton). They further listed:

picture frames	*mantels*
patent medicines	*mince meat*
pleasure carriages	*nails*
awnings	*rubber stamps*
pretzels	*sewer pipe*
band instruments	*shirts*
barber supplies	*umbrellas*
brooms	*typewriters*
coffins	*stained glass*
cigars	*silks*
sun bonnets	*leather*
revolvers	*lime*
organs	*liquor*

and many other practical products.

"Harrisburg has everything to make it the greatest inland city of Pennsylvania," they concluded, and promised "that's what it's going to be before the decade closes."

Professor William H. Wilson's history of Harrisburg's "City Beautiful" movement, published recently in *Pennsylvania History*, shows why the newsboys were so exuberant and how their town became a modern metropolis after 1900. His main points are that the movement was well-planned by prominent private citizens, and that their good plans were executed by private experts, with public money.

Mira Lloyd Dock's speech to the Board of Trade on December 20, 1900, started the spree. Her show of 100 stereoptican slides compared Harrisburg's "hideous conditions" to the good taste of Milwaukee, Boston, and European cities. She also emphasized "the cash value of cleanliness and beauty," insuring a good chance of success for her recommended reforms.

Mira Lloyd Dock, born into wealth, early on tired of music, art, and the other subjects young ladies of good family were expected to devote themselves to. She became an ardent and effective proponent of environmentalism and women's liberation (although that is not what it was called 80 years ago). Her Civic Club was instrumental in the election of Vance McCormick in 1902 and the subsequent transformation of the city. (HSDC)

The election of 1902 concentrated almost entirely on the environment and the quality of life in Harrisburg. The good guys (who won) were reformers like Vance McCormick (who became mayor) and J. Horace McFarland—with Mira Dock an acknowledged presence behind the scenes (where it was said a lady belonged). This streetcar with its banners rolled around Harrisburg on election day, clanging citizens to awareness. Courtesy, McFarland Papers (PHMC)

In April 1901, the *Telegraph* began headlining on the front page its support for city improvements and beautification. There should be "parks, pure water, paved streets, a city hall." A campaign for a bond issue was led by J. Horace McFarland, Mira Dock, and 19 other respectable burghers who were mostly mainstream Protestants, Republicans, well-educated, and relatively young—the average about 40 years of age. The coming election of Vance McCormick in 1902 would assure mayoral support. In Professor Wilson's words, "the elite would assume its class responsibility," for they never doubted that "physical improvement would elevate the urban population." True utilitarians, they would promote the greatest good for the greatest number, (or at least what the campaigners thought was good for them, as there is no record of the greatest number being asked exactly what they wanted.)

A private fund was established to retain expert advice, and the campaigners firmly buttonholed the elite for donations. Wilson quotes McFarland as saying, "men with nothing to do but run big industries"—such as John Reynders, Superintendent of Pennsylvania Steel—"came into your office and looked pleasant until you cashed up, or signed up." The campaigners then controlled this fund, and thus the planning. Engineers and architects were brought in and put to work. James Fuertes of New York took charge of the river, water, and sewage plans, M.R. Sherred of Newark handled streets, and Warren Manning of Boston, a friend of Dock and McFarland, designed parks and boulevards.

With sound plans in hand, the campaigners now called themselves the Harrisburg League for Municipal Improvement, and convinced city council to submit a $1,090,000 bond issue for approval at the next election in February 1902. The League opened an office downtown, began raising more money for publicity, and recruited ordinary citizens to join up, charging $1.00 for membership. They had public meetings, invited questions, and provided answers, because some opposition to their plans was appearing. According to Wilson, skeptics argued that this "Front Street Scheme" would raise taxes and rents as well as elevate the moral tone. The League had local youth deliver leaflets to every home in the city, broadsides that called their opponents "tight-fisted clams." The Civic Club, headquarters for the city's active women, got behind the League and more stereoptican shows were put on. The state legislature cooperated by proposing to move the capital back to Philadelphia unless Harrisburg freshened up, and nature assisted too, by overflowing Paxton Creek in

The E.G. Hoover Jewelry Store was a Harrisburg institution until the 1980s. Its longest business interruption came a few years earlier when the Penn Harris Hotel next to it was demolished. By accident part of the hotel fell on the jewelry store. (HSDC)

A group of prosperous Harrisburg businessmen began the Poor Man's Fishing Club on the Susquehanna in the 1890s. (HSDC)

December and January, fortuitously demonstrating the need for flood control.

According to Wilson, the League also tried a little quiet manipulation of public opinion before the election:

Its members investigated how drinking water from the sewage-laden Susquehanna was affecting the incidence of typhoid, and were dismayed to learn of no dramatic increase in the disease. They did discover lax reporting among local physicians. The doctors were encouraged to bring their reports up to date in January. The result was a manufactured typhoid "epidemic" of thirty cases in one month, double the number of the previous quarter. After the successful bond issue campaign in February the reported cases dropped to nine and in March they fell to four.

The election of February 18, 1902, was a slick victory. The bond issue was passed by two out of three voters, 7,319 to 3,729. Middle class wards approved it more strongly than working class wards, but there was no denying the widespread support.

By 1915 the improvements had been installed. Parkland had increased from 46 to 958 acres. A 140-acre lake was created. The river was deepened by a dam, and concrete steps three miles long were built on the banks. Island Park, one of 11 new parks, had athletic fields and a grandstand. There was a nine-hole golf course in Reservoir Park. Seventy-four miles of roads were now paved, up from about four miles in 1902. The city had filtered water, intercepting sewers, and better flood control. Another $1,341,000 in bonds had been approved for public works. Meanwhile, the city's population had grown from 51,000 to 73,000, and working privately, McFarland and Herman Miller had developed lovely Bellevue Park.

McFarland announced that no other city in the country had done so many valuable things at once, so "harmoniously" and so reliant "upon the plans of experts." Knowing what the burghers wanted to hear, he said Harrisburg was "a made-over town with a degree of efficiency" that reminded him of "the average German city."

As a direct result of the election of 1902, citizens of Harrisburg stopped drinking and bathing directly in the water of the Susquehanna. Some of the work required to complete the civic water system is pictured here, as workers lay pipe to a filtration house. (HSDC)

Bunting decorates a Locust Street commercial building, still standing today, decorated for the dedication of the new capitol in 1906. (HSDC)

It is Professor Wilson's final judgement, however, that by 1915 Harrisburg's "City Beautiful" movement had tired as well as triumphed. J. Horace McFarland had continued to lead but was continually frustrated, being forced to "meddle" rather than manage. As a member of the Park Commission, McFarland felt surrounded by dunces, according to Wilson. McFarland told Dock, " . . . [they] didn't know a pine from a pumpkin. . . ." (At one time he had had to rescue his sacred shade trees from being toppled by the workmen laying sewers.) The President of the Park Commission let billboards be put on his own property even after McFarland offered to match the advertising revenues if the President would desist. McFarland said he

"upset a scheme . . . to girdle Front Street by a trolley line," but found one of his own civic associates had been behind it. He and another park commissioner, one M. Harvey Taylor, did not get along well. McFarland considered Taylor a man whose "dignity" consisted of "running a cigar store." As their last snub, his opponents left McFarland off the new Planning Commission in 1914.

City planning would continue after 1915 in Harrisburg, but it would be headed for the "City Practical" more than the "City Beautiful." Still, the old improvers had built even better than they knew, and they showed the progressive's neatest skill: how to organize.

This truck being used by the Harrisburg Transfer Company was a "Morton Truck built in Harrisburg." Like many communities, Harrisburg had a small automotive industry at the turn of the century. (HSDC)

X
ALIENS IN ISRAEL

In the age of American industry, Pennsylvania forged both swords and plowshares or anything else of iron and steel, making engines, locomotives, and rails for them to run on, electrical equipment, automobile accessories, and machines to make machines. Pittsburgh became the largest center of metal production in the world, and the great furnaces in Steelton, just outside Harrisburg, were rarely cool. Great fortunes, great organizations, and great factories grew up together, all propelled by great gangs of labor.

Most of the men who worked in Steelton in 1911 were not born Americans. They were recent immigrants, taking the Statue of Liberty's calling seriously. From 1900 to 1910, nearly nine million came to this country. Leopold Stokowski, about to be appointed Musical Director of the Philadelphia Orchestra, was an immigrant too, but the steel men had little in common with him, for they would be conducted by the rhythms of the mills, and stare at smokestacks instead of batons. They changed the construction and composition of this country forever, and became the base, eventually, of the new cities, new politics, and new economy. They equipped us for two world wars and won them both.

Ultimately they were Steelton—company town, manufacturer of new Americans, cathedral of blood iron trade, stacked houses facing the fires that grow bones for tall buildings, reminder that all of us were once outsiders.

In 1911 the United States Immigration Commission published 42 volumes of information on the effects of immigration on America, especially on industry. From a portion of the Commission's report *Immigrants in Industries, Part 2: Iron and Steel*, we discover that the commissioners believed that the nation's future would depend on the assimilation of the "new" immigrants from southern and eastern Europe, just as they believed that the nation's past had depended on the assimilation of the "old" immigrants from northern and western Europe. But the report found that the new immigrants were not assimilating, were not "melting" in the pot of public life. The Serbs, Croats, Bulgarians from Macedonia, Slovenes, Magyars, Jews, Poles, Slovaks—often just referred to in the newspapers as "Slavs" or "Austrians"—were still peasants under their workclothes.

To be sure, the commissioners

Charles M. Schwab, president of Bethlehem Steel in the early 1900s, had a vital role in the expansion of the steel industry. His decisions profoundly affected the development of Steelton and many other Pennsylvania towns. From Cirker, Dictionary of American Portraits *(Dover: 1967)*

were proud that America had received new immigrants that were "the strongest, the most enterprising, and the best of their class." They were officially happy that even the new immigrants' "racial and physical characteristics do not survive under the new social and climatic environment of America."

The good results aside, however, the Commission saw the need for a plan to exclude the new immigrants, if not eliminate them. Enough immigration was enough, the commissioners concurred. Their report pronounced that "the American people, as in the past," would continue to "welcome the oppressed" to the Promised Land, but henceforth, they recommended, immigration should be "such both in quality and quantity as not to make too difficult the process of assimilation." Future laws on the "admission of aliens should be based primarily upon economic or business considerations touching the prosperity and well-being of our people." Such laws would repeal "the natural incentive to treat the immigration movement from the standpoint of sentiment." No sentiment need be lost on the new immigrants in any case, asserted the commissioners, because they were not "oppressed":

. . . emigration from Europe is not now an absolute economic necessity, and as a rule those who emigrate to the United States are impelled by a desire for betterment rather than the necessity of escaping intolerable conditions.

The Commission thus proposed laws that would exclude "those unable to read or write in some language," exclude "unskilled laborers unaccompanied by wives

or families," and increase "the amount of money required to be in possession of the immigrant." Furthermore, they proposed that "any alien who becomes a public charge within three years after his arrival should be subject to deportation." The commissioners had built a tight case, on paper, against the new aliens. Eventually, embodied in the Immigration Act of 1924, the commissioners' restrictive sentiments severely rationed immigration from southern and eastern Europe and stopped it altogether from the Orient.

The United States Immigration Commission report of 1911 is relevant to the history of Greater Harrisburg because its rationale came partly from the Commission's study of Steelton, contained in volume eight. The commissioners believed they saw some of the worst effects of the new immigration in that town's rugged life, a miniature of the feudal old world they knew America must never be.

Professor John Bodnar's analysis of the Commission's report, covered in his book *Immigration and Industrialization: Ethnicity in an American Mill Town, 1870-1940*, shows, for example, that Steelton's

City elementary schools were seldom coeducational in the years before World War I, as attested to by this unidentified class in 1910. (HSDC)

Opposite top: *In the early 1900s cars were a rare sight in the country north of Harrisburg. A note attached to this photograph suggests that the cars belonged to historically minded Harrisburghers who were on an exploratory trip to the countryside. (HSDC)*

Opposite bottom: *Driving a coach and four was a gentleman's sport. A group of Harrisburg gentlemen visit Gettysburg in this 1910 photo. (HSDC)*

housing was precisely segregated in 1910. The native-born whites, Irish, and Germans all lived mixed together north of Front Street on the West Side. Blacks and Jews had neighborhoods of their own north of Front Street across from the steel mill. At the "Lower End," still north of Front Street, lived most of the Italians and Slovenes and the bulk of the Serbs and Croats. South of Front Street, in between the railroad tracks and the canal and just west of the mill, lived all the Bulgarians and the remainder of the Serbs and Croats— the "foreign part" of town, according to the local newspaper. This segregation had settled down on Steelton between 1880 and 1910. In 1880 no one living in Steelton had been born in southern or eastern Europe. By 1910 Italians, Slovenians, and Croatians were one-third of the town's population, and more than one-half of the steel mill's workforce.

Jobs and wages were just as precisely segregated in the mill by 1910. Where working conditions were the harshest, there one found the most foreign-born and black workers, and where conditions were less harsh, there one found the fewest ethnics. Bodnar writes,

In 1902 five "Austrians"—Jurovic, Marovoich, Gatis, Muza, and Radjanovic—were burned to death "in a horrible manner" when molten metal from the open hearth poured on them. In 1906 Anton Pijac, a boy of sixteen, fell through the top of a gas oven and was cremated.... The list of victims in 1907 speaks for itself: Tesak, Pajolic, Stifko, Knukle, Termer, Petruti, Pierce, Oconicke, Ukelic, Krameric, Szep, Peffer, Gross, Susic, Restoff, Trajbarico, Polanec, Turnbaugh, and Pugar.

Nearly 80 percent of all the native whites were skilled workers earning more than $1.50 per day in 1910. About 59 percent of the native blacks were in that category. Approximately 47 percent of the Slovenians, 34 percent of the Croatians, 14 percent of the Serbians, and 8 percent of the Bulgarians were skilled workers making that rate of pay. All the remainder of the eastern Europeans were unskilled workers making less than $1.50 per day. The average unskilled immigrant earned 11 cents an hour. The ore shovels were called "Hunky banjos." Of 136 foremen, 117 were Americans, Germans, or Irish. And according to Bodnar, the immigrants would not rise from rags to riches very soon: "The distinctive characteristic of Steelton's work force from 1880 to 1925 was career immobility."

The commissioners found that social segregation in Steelton was coupled with ethnic antagonism. Their report said there was "general deprecation" of the immigrants rather than "open hostility." Copying down some of the native white's stereotyping (and engaging in a little of their own), the commissioners wrote,

The Magyars are regarded as the most effective laborers on the general labor force. They drink more alcoholic liquor than the Macedonians, but less than the Slavs, and are considered more trustworthy than the latter. The South Italians ... are active, but less industrious than the Croatians, and less able to endure high temperatures ... [the Italians] have a poor reputation for trustworthiness. The Macedonians are conscientious plodders, willing to do the work required of them, but ineffective through awkwardness ... The negro is

1
2
3
4
5
6
7

Horace McFarland, author, rosarian, and businessman, sits on a rise amidst a growth of virgin hemlock trees at Fort Hunter. McFarland was instrumental in founding the rose garden near Polyclinic Hospital. (HSDC)

no longer a factor in the general labor gang . . . strange to say, he is unable to endure the intense and steady heat of the open hearth . . .

"The American laborer does not care to work with the 'Hunkie'," observed the commissioners, who decided it was best to douse the flame before the lid blew off the melting pot.

American laborers' opinions of the "Hunkies" had not been kept a secret. In 1905 the Order of United American Mechanics' Steelton chapter, an organization of native white skilled workers, issued the following proclamation:

Whereas, the record of immigration shows that more than 800,000 foreign-born persons landed upon American soil during the past year—not the stur-

dy people who came before the sixties to find a place where they might worship God according to the dictates of their own conscience, to build homes for themselves . . . but from pauper districts of Southern Europe . . . the incubators of nihilism, anarchy, disease, and crime . . .

Therefore, be it resolved that we demand enactment of such laws as will shield us from the depressing effects of unrestricted immigration, to the end that the American laborer may not only be protected against the product of foreign pauper laborer, but that we may be protected against direct competition in our own country by the incoming of the COMPETITIVE ALIEN—the foreign pauper laborers themselves.

It is Bodnar's judgement, however, that the Anglo-Saxon leadership of Steelton was ultimately more interested in controlling the new immigrants than in condemning them. He writes,

Ethnic communities could remain as long as immigrants cleaned neighborhoods, ceased particular ethnic customs such as parading, limited their drinking, learned the lessons of Protestant Christianity, memorized patriotic songs, spoke English, voted Republican, and above all, were thrifty and content.

The aliens' response to "general deprecation," was to "turn inward and occupy themselves with their own problems," says Bodnar. They organized fraternal associations and churches based on ethnicity and kinship, and waited for the day their children would inherit the earth beyond the hearth.

Now Steelton's best days are gone, the youngsters sigh, but the worst days too, the elders say.

IRON WORKS OF THE McCORMICK ESTATE AT HARRISBURG, PA.

NEW YORK DAILY GRAPHIC — MAY 3, 1878

The iron and steel industries became important to Dauphin County before the Civil War. The post-Civil War years saw the flowering of the family-owned operations. Iron and steel strengthened the fortunes of such local families as the Camerons and the McCormicks. (HSDC)

Wistar Iron Works, shown in this late 19th century photo, stood along the Pennsylvania canal. A producer of pig iron, it was typical of the many independent iron and steel mills that developed in the Harrisburg area. (HSDC)

Dressed for gym at the age of about ten, Cub Houston sported a white shirt, black trousers, black stockings, and high-button gym shoes. Courtesy, Cub Houston

XI
CUB'S RAGTIME

When did modern times begin? Some historians say America has always been a modern society, that it never had to overthrow Old World ways. Others say old times here were forgotten after the Civil War, after Americans had faced the facts of total conflict and whole populations had fought one another, not just professional soldiers meeting on a field of honor. Still others say modern times began after World War I, after Americans had sensed that President Wilson's "war to end all wars" led mainly to their intermission, when radios and cars began to occupy so many of our hours, and shocking new forms of creativity signaled a new sensibility, when men and women ceased to wear only dark clothes and to think only the brightest thoughts.

All three dates are persuasive, but especially the last one. Examining life in 1917 specifically, one can see the last light of innocence just before the dawn of modern doubt. By 1917, 24 states had voted to prohibit alcohol, completing the ultimate Victorian reform, but Margaret Sanger had just opened America's first birth control clinic in Brooklyn, defying the ultimate Victorian taboo. Norman Rockwell had just begun to illustrate covers for the Saturday Evening Post, *creating a remarkable reservoir of images of the traditional good life, yet "Dada" artists were executing works of "meaningful nothing, where nothing has any meaning." In 1917 old-fashioned ideas dominated the new movies—"Birth of a Nation," "The Tramp," and "The Perils of Pauline" reassured everyone that romance and bravery were still reliable, but James Joyce and D.H. Lawrence were writing novels that Harriet Beecher Stowe and Sir Walter Scott would have never imagined.*

This time in between the past and the future, the maudlin and the modern, was a ragtime, and in this chapter "Cub" Huston's own marvelous snapshot of his growing up in Harrisburg before World War I shows a city in the last years of its own childhood.

Harrisburg had a ragtime before the Great War. We can know something of it—at least a child's fine time of it—because Ralph "Cub" Huston, born in 1907, raised and living in Harrisburg today, has written down his ragtime from memory. His concrete particulars of porch swings and candy counters are antiques for us now. His details bespeak a lost city that was occasionally cosmopolitan but usually a congestion of little communities, and citizens who were quite conscious of one's social class and native country but still congenial. Such facts show us how it *felt* to live then. Other boys from unluckier streets would have different memories to tell us. Still, read a little of his "No—Back and Over" as it is, full of realism, nostalgia, and humanity, and enjoy.

"Early in the 1900s row houses were built. Although they all looked alike, each had its own roofed porch separated from the next neighbor by a rail fence. These porches were wide enough to have a three or four-person swing on which cushions were used to make it more comfortable. Smaller homes and those on narrow streets did not enjoy the luxury of porches, but they did have their steps. Steps were used as gathering places for family and friends. They were the original air conditioners, libraries, school rooms, romantic nooks, and forums for discussion. They were home base for games, and a desert island if you thought so. They were privilege for good deportment, as well as prison for misbehaving.

"After supper the whole neighborhood would sit out front. First came the kids, and then, when the dishes were washed and dried, the grown-ups came out. If there were too many to squeeze comfortably in the space, chairs or benches were moved onto the sidewalks. Everyone did it. On most of the narrow streets or alleys the sidewalks were as proportionately narrow, so one could get more air by moving the chair out on the street. The street sitters faced the house and rested their feet on the curbing.

"The steps were wide enough to take care of all eight in our family. Mama and Papa, five kids, and Aunt Mira, who lived with us. Papa was the provider of all this, but he really didn't have much chance to use either the porch or the bench. He worked 16 hours a day. He did have Wednesday nights and every other Friday afternoon and Sunday nights off. Our Mothers used wood or coal ranges, and what martyrs our Mothers were. In those days everyone had to have hot meals or you would not survive. The stoves were kept going for three hots, starting with oatmeal and eggs for breakfast. Three meals a day plus making beds, washing, ironing, baking, emptying slop jars, sewing, helping with lessons, taking care of the sick and old people, and still loving. That was Mother.

"Grocers had long, hard days. They opened their stores at six or seven in the morning. Men coming from their nightshifts would stop to buy the things that had been written on a list the night before. The grocer's day continued until late at night. Neighborhood stores were seldom longer than a home living room; in fact, many were located in what would have been the parlor. Yet, in that small space you could find everything a family would need for survival.

"Strange as it now seems, not very

much was pre-packaged. Flour and sugar were delivered to the store in barrels, and you could buy as much as you wanted. Other things came to the grocer in barrels, such as cod, vinegar, pickles, and crackers. Lard came in wooden buckets, and barrels of coal oil and molasses were kept in the grocer's cellar or an adjoining shed. Molasses was no problem in warm weather, but in cold weather it was a real job to draw a pint or quart. Customers bringing oil cans to be filled would usually leave them on the sidewalk as they entered the store. This was done to make sure the order for other things would not smell of oil.

After the grocer filled an oil can, he usually plugged the spout with a potato so that the oil would not spill on the way home.

"In groceries you found out that everything was not odorless, colorless, or tasteless. Entering you could smell coffee, tea, bananas, apples, pickles, smoked meats, coal oil, peanut butter, limburger cheese, and candy.

"Although corner groceries were scattered all over the city, most every family, rich and poor alike, went to market. This was a way of life, and what an experience. In Harrisburg, the markets were open on Wednesdays and Saturdays, from

The Harrisburg Public Library had the state's first bookmobile. Painted bright red and nicknamed "the Cardinal," it went into operation in 1925. These Harrisburg students would wait in line to use it. Courtesy, Dauphin County Library System

early in the morning until about nine at night. Uptowners generally went to Broad, Central City and Shipokers to Chestnut, and Hillers to Allison. Occasionally lines would be crossed, but not very often.

"You left home with wicker baskets. Paper bags were not plentiful, and those used had been used before and saved for the next market. Our family was a three-basket one. Baskets became heavier and heavier as you did your buying. At first you would hold them with your hand until your fingers would swell; then you used your arm until ridges would appear on your skin. You would change from one arm to the other until it really didn't matter—they both hurt.

"Practically all the sellers were real farmers or real butchers. In season, each stall would have lettuce, endive, carrots, turnips, beets, eggs, tomatoes, potatoes, cabbage, celery, and corn. These were regular items. Then there were special seasons, including one with the most delectable, sweetest strawberries in the entire world from York County. You could look at a stall and tell which farmers were from York County by the looks of their berries. Country sounds were also heard: roosters crowing, geese honking, and ducks quacking. You

would see people leaving the market carrying one or more live chickens by their feet. Dressed chickens were displayed with the yellow fat extending from the innards. This would help the buyers know how much flavor could be expected.

"Markets also provided opportunities for boys to earn money. Those of us having wagons would park outside the entrances and bid for the chance to haul the baskets to the homes of the shoppers. You had no set rate, as you were at the mercy of the customer. You learned the tricks of the trade. You learned to tip your cap, smile at the right time, how to be careful at curbs, and how to show appreciation. You also learned which customers were generous, and which ones to avoid if you could. On good days you could earn more than a dollar. . . .

"The Gods with barrels of ambrosia were not any richer than a kid with a penny in a candy store. With a penny one had a choice of a most wonderful assortment. Perhaps the most difficult decisions we made in our lifetime were those made in front of candy counters. You would feast your eyes from left to right, from right to left, from front to back, and even diagonally. You had to decide not only on taste, but also on which items gave the

Most market houses were little more than sheds that provided shelter for farmers' stalls. Some rural sites in Pennsylvania still have open markets. Their foods, however, are usually fresher and better tasting than the prepackaged provender of supermarkets. (HSDC)

Opposite: Cub does not tell us how many other 15-year-old Harrisburghers were tempted by the pipe guardrail atop the old YMCA building. In any case, Cub himself stood there with the dome of the new Capitol in the background while a friend recorded the event. Courtesy, Cub Houston

Patriotic floats were a staple of Memorial Day parades. This 1912 float recalls the War of 1812. (HSDC)

most for your money. There were four-fors, three-fors, two-fors, and the more expensive one-for. We had to choose from sour balls, orange bananas, cocoanut strips or straps, all kinds of assorted chocolates and cordials, caramels, Necco wafers, jujubes, peppermint sticks, hard cherries on wire, and cherries in chocolate. There were long, thin glass tubes, or straws filled with multi-colored beads of sugar. If you wanted something to last a long time, you usually picked sour balls or lollypops. Boys had fun buying licorice, because they could emulate their elders by pretending they were chewing tobacco.

"Private and public horse stables were located throughout Harrisburg. Many of the wealthy along Front Street had stables on their own property. Others less affluent, but still able to own one or more horses, stabled them away from their homes. Horses pulled surries, sedans, cabs, buggies, and runabouts. There were delivery wagons, carts, milk and ice wagons, hearses, brewery and huckster wagons. There were pony carts and junk wagons. There were hundreds of them. Horses were broken to the wagon, but not street broken. Street cleaners were necessary for the health and appearance of the community. I will never forget the aroma of brewery horse urine. From a health standpoint, I am glad it has disappeared with other things, but it was distinctive and more acceptable than automobile gas fumes.

Irving College, a women's college, expired early in the 20th Century. Its buildings still stand in Mechanicsburg, but they are now apartments. (PHMC)

"Every parade worth watching had its horses. What a variety of parades. Memorial Day, Fourth of July, Labor Day, Election, Patriotic, School, Circus and Columbus Day, minstrel shows and conventions were all occasions for parades. The inauguration of the Governor brought out a whole company of mounted State Police. What steeds they had and what riders the Police were! When they passed the onlookers applauded, not only because of their appearance, but also as a gesture of appreciation for the job they did. The Police made sure citizens were protected. They were tough men, but gentlemen.

"Circus parades were fantastic. Their bands played a different kind of music. It was loud and fast. Circus horses were fascinating. Teams of matched pairs, fours, sixes, and eights pulled the wagons. Drivers had up to eight pairs of reins in their hands. Their real skill became apparent when they showed how they could manipulate turning corners. Circus wagons were perhaps the most highly decorated vehicles ever seen by man. Animals from the circus menagerie were included in parades. There were lions, tigers, bears, hyenas, and others. Camels were led by men dressed as Arabs. The last thing in a circus parade was the calliope, the only enjoyable out-of-tune instrument in the world. The notes seemed to explode in your ears, and they meant the end of the greatest free show on earth.

"Great names of the theatre world included Harrisburg in their stops. Howard Thurston, the great magician, was usually scheduled for performances at the Orpheum Theatre for the week between Christmas and New Year's. He also gave a free performance for orphans and underprivileged kids at Fahnestock Hall in the old YMCA. It was his custom to have one of the boys from the Y help in a couple of his acts. I was chosen and acted as his stooge.

"I am somewhat clumsy, and yet I appeared with the great Pavlova. A couple of my pals and I were offered fifty cents apiece to put on gunny sacks and act as peasants in one of her scenes. It was the easiest money I ever earned. All we had to do was sit in a group as this graceful lady danced around us. Someone from the cast applied make-up to our faces. I wore mine home to show my folks.

"Another popular, almost yearly, visitor to Harrisburg was Lyman Howe. He was a world traveler who took motion pictures and then narrated them as he showed them. To appreciate the impact his presentations had on us, it must be remembered that geography lessons told little of customs, people, or scenery. Howe's lectures and the *National Geographic* magazine were our only real contacts with the rest of the world.

"Father T.B. Johnson was assigned

to St. Patrick's Cathedral as the Assistant Pastor. To the neighborhood kids he was Roman Catholic, Lutheran, Methodist, Presbyterian, and Jewish. He was White and he was Black. Everyone knew him and everyone loved him. Although he was not physically large, he was a ball of fire. He played baseball and touch football with us. When there was a death, sickness, or misfortune in the neighborhood, the first person to call on the family was usually Father Johnson. When good fortune came, he was there to congratulate. To him, denominations or sects were names only. If he saw differences between religions and races, he didn't show it.

''One time a few of his parishioners thought the hat he was wearing was too shabby and not proper for a man of the cloth. They took up a collection among themselves and bought Father Johnson a new, fine-looking one. Within a day or two the Reverend was again wearing his old, shabby hat. One of the donors asked the good man about this, and he humbly replied that he had given the new hat to some poor man who didn't own one. 'You see,' said Father Johnson, 'I had two hats, but only one small head.' When this saintly man was transferred to another out-of-town

As he grew, Cub enjoyed the adventures that enlivened the days of adolescents about 100 years ago. When he was about 13, he and his friend Junior Forrer captured (and presumably dispatched) a copperhead—an event sufficiently momentous to call for a photograph. Courtesy, Cub Houston

parish, something went out of our lives with him.

"James Bruner was a black butler for Mrs. Lyman D. Gilbert. I suppose I was five or six years old when we first became acquainted. Although 20 or more years passed from our first meeting to our last, he was the only one I have known who didn't change in manner or appearance. He was well-groomed, kindly, gracious in manner, polite, concerned, and he always had the warmest smile. The Governor's mansion was one block away from the Gilbert residence. It was common in those days to see a distinguished Governor walking about town. Many of them knew James and would stop and chat with him as he swept the sidewalk or trimmed the hedge. He looked like a fashion plate even while doing these chores.

"Living as close to Front Street as we did, the word 'rich' became a part of our early vocabulary. We used the word in many ways, but seldom with rancor. In reputation of character, some of the rich were paupers, but that was their business. Perhaps local residents knew of the few indiscretions, but knowing, paid little or no attention. Some of the rich were first-class snobs, but like those who were rumored to have had indiscretions, we could ignore or forget them.

"Lyman Gilbert came to our house one day and said he and Mrs. Gilbert were going on an extended trip. He wanted our family to move into their home and live there while they were gone. He said, 'You know, John, with your youngsters around and using our furniture and rugs, the moths won't get into things.' My Dad thought awhile and replied, 'That's right, Lyman, but what would keep the moths away from ours?'

"I am sure that I knew the names of everyone in all the streets in our neighborhood before going to first grade. These people also knew me and where I lived. You learned which ones would smile, wave, or greet you. These were by far the majority. Then there were others who were born crabs and didn't change as long as they lived. You shared your neighbors' difficulties and were glad when nice things happened to them. Your walks were saddened at times by seeing crepes on some doors. These homes were hard to pass by, whether you knew the deceased or not. You just did not feel good when you saw a crepe.

"Within three blocks on our particular street were Whites, Negroes, Italians, Germans, Swedes, English, Jews, and Irish. Before anyone gets the idea that all living was peaches and cream, it should be understood that we had our fights and misunderstandings. We had teacher's pets, sissies, and roughnecks. We had religious and race differences, but all these were subject to change on short notice. We called some of the Jews we were sore at 'Christ Killers,' but these same guys invited us to their Bar Mitzvah ceremonies. One of the boys had an Uncle in the German Army. This boy and other members of his family were not warmly accepted during the War. There was nothing wrong with the boy or his family, other than their being German. It must have been lonely for them during this period.

"As kids we never knew that the whole world was not the same as Liberty Street, nor did we care. These people were our friends, our cronies, our teammates, our life."

Even as a boy of four or five, Cub Houston took to the outdoor life. Here he displays some fish he evidently caught himself. His clothing was standard for a boy of his day, including black stockings, high button shoes, and (Houston points out specifically) pants . . . not knickers. Courtesy, Cub Houston

An ad for "The Busy Bee" shows the waiters, countermen, and owners ready to serve food in their modern, 1920s establishment. (PHMC)

XII
THE BOTTOM LINE

*America and Greater Harrisburg were coming of age together in the Twenties. Charles Lindbergh flew the Atlantic in 1927; Harrisburg shared its first airport with York in 1930. The first commercially sponsored radio program was broadcast from New York City in 1922; Radio Station WHP turned on in Harrisburg in 1924. Notre Dame's "Four Horsemen" upset Army in football in 1924; Harrisburg Tech claimed the national high school championship in 1919, scoring 701 points to none for its opponents. The team from John Harris High went undefeated from 1929 to 1931. The "Charleston" was the step to dance in America in 1925; George Reist's Dance Boat was the place to whirl in Harrisburg. In a sensational trial in Chicago, Nathan Leopold and Richard Loeb were convicted of the "thrill killing" of little Bobby Frank in 1924; the murder of Verna Klink was Harrisburg's sensational crime of 1927. New Yorkers and Harrisburghers were now thumbing through the same magazines (*Time, Readers Digest, *and the* New Yorker *itself), listening to the same music (George Gershwin's "Rhapsody in Blue," Hoagy Carmichael's "Star Dust," and Eddie Cantor's "Makin' Whoopee"), and reading the same books (F. Scott Fitzgerald's* The Great Gatsby, *Ernest Hemingway's* A Farewell to Arms, *and Sinclair Lewis'* Babbitt*).*

It was a good time to take an accounting of city life, because as President Coolidge had said, the business of America was business. How else would we know, but for the Greater Harrisburg Chamber of Commerce's Industrial Survey of 1928, that 146,657 dozen shirts and 46,044,675 "cigar units" were manufactured locally in 1925 (26 stogies per pocket), or that Dauphin County produced 936,702 gallons of ice cream the same year, but that York County made all the cones.

The Chamber's mimeographed report, compiled during February and March 1928, estimated that Harrisburg's population in July would be 86,900, up 1,200 since January. The suburban population was 52,000.

Eighty-eight percent of the city people were native-born whites, seven percent were black, and five percent were foreign-born whites (most of those were from Russia, Italy, Germany, Hungary, England, and Ireland, in that order).

Close to two-thirds of all adults were married. Each family averaged 4.0 members, but each dwelling 4.5 residents.

There were 43,936 members of 81 churches, or about half of all men, women, and children, led by 13,500 Lutherans, 6,259 Methodists, 5,552 Presbyterians, and 5,465 Roman Catholics.

There were 2,040 mules in the county.

There were 33 elementary schools, parochial and public, for 8,800 pupils. Within the city limits there were 13 theaters showing films and vaudeville, 22 hotels, 12 service clubs, and three major newspapers. Four thousand people played in the 1,100 acres of parks each day.

Every 24 hours 142 passenger trains and 126 freight trains passed

Beth-El Temple has served the Jewish community since the late 1920s. (HSDC)

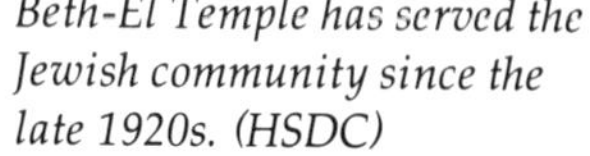

through the city, or about one train every five minutes. During peak hours 87 streetcars ran in the metropolitan area.

Rent for a six-room house started at about $20 a month. A new brick rowhouse could be bought for about $4,000, or $300 down and $50 a month. Sixty percent of all homes were owned in 1927, up from 36 percent in 1920 and almost half of Harrisburg's families had their own telephones.

The city's 16,000 employed men and women made an average wage of $1,300 per year with about 80 percent of all men employed and about 25 percent of all women.

Among the over 2,000 retail establishments in the city were 30 places to buy firewood, coal, and ice, 114 shops selling candy and ice cream, and 250 cigar and tobacco counters. There were 410 corner grocery stores, 51 pool halls, and 56 junk dealers. Harrisburghers spent more money annually on musical instruments than they did on either funerals or gasoline, and they bought more hats than sporting goods. Indeed, they spent more per capita on goods and services than residents of any other county.

The survey pronounced "optimism." Energy from gas and electricity was "unlimited." The city had an "unusually satisfactory labor market." Employers had "no difficulty whatever in securing more labor, both male and female, than they can use." Harrisburg was an "open shop town" and "American-born labor predominated." There was "no serious labor trouble at any time" and "no interference from organizers." Coincidentally, "The church attendance in Harrisburg is high," they said, "which indicates a good class of labor." There was "general order" throughout the city.

Greater Harrisburg's industrial outlook in 1928 was "encouraging," they concluded.

And the Depression came.

In 1919 the Harrisburg Tech football team (right) trounced the Portland, Maine, football team (left) to become national high school champions. A close inspection of the players on both teams, especially Harrisburg's, suggests that either some of the players spent quite some time in high school or else got there late. (HSDC)

Left: *Local breweries once added to a town's sense of community and civic pride. Harrisburg's Fink Brewing Company, like today's beer industry, tried to use the image of an attractive woman to sell their product. This postcard dates to pre-World War I. (PHMC)*

The staff of the Hill Post Office poses with visiting
dignitaries in this late 1930s photo. (HSDC)

XIII
TWO TALES OF A CITY

In Greater Harrisburg and elsewhere, the Thirties were as rough as the Twenties were roaring. The stock market crash of 1929 and the Depression that followed were largely democratic in their effects. In 1930, 1,300 banks closed in the United States; by 1932, 5,000 had closed. Industrial production was at half-volume and so was the total of wages paid. About 12 million Americans, or 25 percent of the workforce, were unemployed. Charles Lindbergh's son was kidnapped, the "Hindenburg" dirigible exploded, and Amelia Earhart's plane disappeared. More than 32,000 Americans were killed in auto accidents in 1938. The 1936 flood in Harrisburg was the worst to date.

But there were silver linings. The New Deal heartened most of the people, even if it didn't stop the Depression. Boulder Dam was completed, the Queen Mary was launched, and the Golden Gate Bridge was opened. The movies were better than ever, maybe the best ever: "It Happened One Night," "Mutiny on the Bounty," "Gone With the Wind" (all Clark Gable triumphs), "Captains Courageous," "Boys Town" (Spencer Tracy's Academy Awards), and "Stagecoach" (John Wayne's opening night). The Forties would start off with "The Grapes of Wrath" and "The Philadelphia Story."

In 1939 the World's Fair opened in New York, showing how the future might be planned. Its theme was the "World of Tomorrow." They planned for the future in Harrisburg that year too, and suffered in the present.

The Municipal League's Report of 1939-1940, "Planning for the Future of Harrisburg," proclaimed the second phase of Greater Harrisburg's improvements. In the main, the area was probably well-served by this report. Malcolm Dill, Resident Regional Planner, and E.S. Draper Associates, Consultants, both employed by President Vance McCormick and Secretary J. Horace McFarland of the Municipal League, had done a professional job. They offered 129 recommendations to modernize the larger metropolitan area, the inner city, and the suburban fringe. Having designed the "City Beautiful" successfully, now the planners and the League would build the "City Practical"—a progressive, well-coordinated, rational place to live that would accommodate Harrisburg's new "automobility."

It seems the planners were "doctoring" a city: in their report's words, they "diagnosed ailments" and wrote "prescriptions." Perhaps it was such hubris that led the planners to say that there was never any "valid reason" for the city's narrow house lots, which led to "endless rows of monotonous houses predominately without architectural merit." Perhaps that judgment bespoke the planners' tastes more than the residents'. The planners stated that these rowhouses would be unattractive "in the eyes of the coming generation, which is witnessing construction of an increasing number of attractive single-family dwellings, set on adequate-sized lots"— not foreseeing the monotony and troublesome ecology of Levittown.

The planners said Harrisburg's housing pattern led to "crowded conditions for automobile parking," especially downtown, where there was "indiscriminate parking" and

A rifle team, in Civil War uniforms, fires a salute for Memorial Day in a Harrisburg cemetery in 1938. (HSDC)

"inexcusable double parking" that would "destroy the value of a lane of moving traffic." But they did not realize that cities made easy for drivers would become cities driven by cars.

The planners insisted that Harrisburg needed "zoning," their "form of publicly-applied insurance against cupidity and selfishness." The planners said the city needed to build new neighborhoods, such as the "Harrisburg Housing Authority's plan for a development for white people between Sycamore and Hanover Streets on 13th Street," not realizing that all "white"

neighborhoods were the problem, not the solution.

The planners said the city should manage its pedestrians better, and recommended "admonition by amplifiers," such as a "not-too-loud-speaker" telling "the young woman in the red hat to wait for the green light." This order "would receive embarrassed compliance." "Technique is important," they said.

They planned, and Greater Harrisburg progressed, but did the consultants ever consult ordinary residents? Dorothy Day, visiting social worker, was not concerned about making the city safe for a Chevy.

The Pennsylvania Railroad introduced the famous GG-1 electric locomotive in 1934. Designed by the great industrial designer Raymond Loewy and engineered by John V.B. Duer, they were so reliable and durable that many are still in service. In Harrisburg during World War II, they were the principal means of intercity travel. (HSDC)

The square in Hummelstown was the scene of the Homecoming Parade in the late 1930s. Hummelstown is typical of the east shore small towns that ring Harrisburg. "Homecoming" was held to welcome natives of the town who had moved away— including those who succumbed to the lure of the big city in Harrisburg. (HSDC)

Toilets bothered her. Reporting to the Catholic magazine *Commonweal* on poverty in Harrisburg, she wrote on July 14, 1939:

Here in Harrisburg there just isn't any toilet. You go next door to the neighbors. And there was no running water until a week ago. Most of the houses on the block have no running water. The neighbors pay one man down the street for the privilege of getting pails of water from his house. Our place, the Blessed Martin Home, is two rooms, now scrubbed clean . . . There is paint and linoleum on the floor, the linoleum donated out of her salary by a colored cook who works all day and comes over to help us in the evening. There is a faucet in the kitchen now, but no sink. We are begging for that.

Her Catholic Workers had given some families the Blessed Martin as a temporary lodging. They put up

Harrisburg's elite has traditionally belonged to either Pine Street or Market Square Presbyterian churches. The Pastor's Aid Society of the Pine Street Church posed at this meeting on May 18, 1934. Mrs. Vance McCormick (second from left) and Mrs. James Cameron (fourth from left) were probably the richest Harrisburg socialites. (HSDC)

"two white families with thirteen and seven children respectively and one colored family with seven children," she wrote.

How they got along in two rooms with no water and no toilet is hard to understand. . . . In one case the children were rolled out of bed and left in their night things as the clothes and bedding were loaded on the van.

Dorothy Day had other saint-simple stories to tell about her Catholic Workers and the poor of Harrisburg, some just too sad in their details, such as the story of "Lucille," whom they found Job-like and dying in an empty house. "Lucille grew up on the streets," Day said. "She and her brothers and sisters just prowled around, living as best they could." Father Kirchner of St. Patrick's baptized and anointed her before she died.

Day observed,

The greatest difficulty in Harrisburg is to find a home to live in, even when a family is on relief and has money to pay rent. Housing seems to be the greatest immediate problem of the city.

The Municipal League planners knew that too, in a way. They began compiling their report that same July. Their recommendation in favor of slum clearance and "eventual Neighborhood Units" said that the "present dwelling shortage, from a social and economic standpoint, has reached a rather serious stage." But there was no room or reason for intimate evidence in their report.

Activities on the "Home Front" give some idea of the enormous national commitment to World War II. In Harrisburg, the local USO (United Service Organization, which was created to boost the morale of service personnel) maintained a Floating Club, moored in the river at Locust Street, where there was dancing to live music every night. (HSDC)

Maris Harve Taylor lived to be over 100 years old, and by the 1960s he was a Harrisburg institution. He is pictured here receiving honors from Governor Scranton for his long service to the public. (PHMC)

XIV
HARVE TAYLOR'S
SECRET DIARY

The post-war history of Greater Harrisburg deserves its own book, for what happened to this area in the last 40 years is what happened to America at large since 1945. Harrisburg's city population climbed to more than 89,000 by 1950, then declined to around 53,000 by 1980. This was also true of other northeastern cities. Greater Harrisburg's suburbs and neighboring towns grew like toadstools on spring bluegrass. This was also true of other cities across the country. Harrisburg struggled to renew itself, and so did Baltimore. Steel and railroads became less prosperous here, and likewise so in Pittsburgh. The place of state government expanded in Harrisburg, as it also did in Albany. The interstate highway system (the largest construction project in the world's history) tied all the major cities together even tighter, and proved again that you have to put your finger on Harrisburg to make the knot. And when the nation or the state were prosperous, Greater Harrisburg was too, usually with one of the lowest unemployment rates in the states.

But as we point out the parallel paths that America and Greater Harrisburg have followed in their recent history, we must be careful not to miss a deeper truth: this area is more notable for its stability than any dynamism up or down. South central Pennsylvania has one of the lowest rates of emigration—people leaving—of any state in the nation. These people don't have their heads in the clouds or in the sand. They are the most middle western of Easterners.

Perhaps the quickest and most penetrating way to cover modern change, and the lack of change, is to try to see it through some observer's eyes. So I have taken the liberty to imagine what Harve Taylor, the quintessential Harrisburgher, might have written in a diary during these years. Who can better represent us—not at our best or at our worst—but at the good balance we would be?

May 3, 1946. Stopped by Shipoke on a good Spring day. Joe and Dom Caldarelli are home from the war now, along with about 7,000 other boys from the area. They moved back in with their folks on Pancake Row. There used to be renters moving in'n'out all the time on the block, but since the war nobody's budged an inch. Roy and Mary Houser are on the corner at 100 Conoy, the nine Snavelys at 102, Ralph and Elsie Schlitzer and their daughter at 104, Henrietta Carroll and her child at 106, the six Shearers at 108, the nine O'Keefes at 110, Ross and Mary Hart at 112, and Vince and Carrie Caldarelli and their two heroes at 114, across the street from where I was born. That's about 4 baseball teams squeezed in between home plate and second base. When I grew up here you never had the privacy to be lonely. And when your neighbor had bread, everybody had bread.

December 25, 1949. Merry Christmas, and John O'Hara's novel present to us this year was *A Rage to Live.* Everybody's been tryin' to figure out who's who and what's what in it. I'm not sure how many local friends he'll have left when this is over, but I'd bet he'll know more lawyers.

January 25, 1952. Well, they dedicated "me" today. What does it mean when they name a bridge after you while you're still alive? If it's the thought that counts, that's what worries me! Ha! I told them I would do my very best to keep living up to this honor.

March 3, 1957. Today they announced they'll tear down the old County Prison at Walnut and Court. I remember back in the Gay Nighties when they locked you up in there if you even looked at loitering. More than a thousand guys arrested one year. I'm surprised the joint didn't fall down back then from the sheer weight of all that civic concern.

January 19, 1958. They opened up the new Jewish Community Center up on Front Street today. They opened up their own country club, the Blue Ridge, about 20 years ago after they found out every other place was restricted. There's a real story there—what the Jews have done for this town, even though they didn't owe us many favors.

June 18, 1958. Get packed! They're going to clear the slums! About 200 houses and stores are going to be bulldozed in Shipoke to make way for the South Bridge and the ramps—80 on Race Street and everything south of Tuscarora. And they're taking down about 180 houses up at 6th and Boas. You can't say they aren't trying to do their leveling best.

July 21, 1958. There were 89,554 people in Harrisburg in 1950, about 93,000 in 1957, and today the *Evening News* predicted there'll be

Harve Taylor was at the height of his influence in the 1950s when he posed for this and innumerable other pictures with Dauphin County worthies. (PHMC)

The State Theatre was Harrisburg's last movie palace. In the 1970s the theater was torn down and Locust Court replaced it. (PHMC)

At the turn of the century, Shipoke was decidedly a working-class neighborhood. The eight-to-ten-room houses were too small to accommodate a middle-class family and its necessary corps of servants. Conoy Street at the corner of Front (south of the section where Front Street is a busy thoroughfare) was dusty and quiet. Courtesy, Michael Barton

In recent years, the eastern side of Shipoke has been obliterated by Interstate 83 and its ramps, but the western part has become an enclave for people united by a common fondness for living in houses in an urban area. The houses along Conoy Street remain attractive, some because of continuous maintenance, others because of restoration. New sidewalks and paving make the place less dusty than in earlier times. Courtesy, Michael Barton

97,000 in 1965 and 100,000 in 1975. I won't bet you can expect Republicans to be that prolific. Now Democrats, that's another thing.

July 28, 1961. Paul Beers wrote in the paper about Front Street today. The street went one-way in 1956, the Wallower Mansion (once Harrisburg Academy) started to come down in 1959, the old Governor's Mansion in 1960, and now on Front from Division to Market it's about half commercial where all the big homes used to be. Maybe Second Streeters are behind this. Better view of the river over the parking lots.

November 7, 1964. What can I say? We got beat, that's what. At least I did it in the primary and missed the rush. But Nibs Franklin brought his ward in for the Grand Old Party. The Goldwater Blacks, they are, the only Negro ward in the country to go Republican this year. That's the party of Lincoln for you.

June 23, 1969. Trouble up on Allison Hill today, big trouble. Race trouble. There are two main problems in Harrisburg—white people and black people.

January 24, 1972. The boys will say Pop-Pop's got it made now, because today I'm in the *New York Times.* Their reporter Homer Bigart came in to report on our "Hairy Seven" trial. You know, there's more radicals in this town than you'd think, and they run their own newspaper. Not bad. Anyway, they naturally sent Homer to see me to find out what makes the place tick. I said to him, "You say your name's Homer Big-City?" He asked me what Harrisburg thought about Vietnam, and I said Front Street supports Nixon but Shipoke is against it because they "don't want their sons drafted and because they want to live on relief." That's the way he quoted me. Hope nobody in Shipoke reads the *Times.* Mainly because he spelled it "Shypoke." I bet somebody told Homer that waterbird story. You don't see "Shite-poke" in the paper anymore.

May 7, 1972. They opened up the new Hersheypark today. What a park! What a town. Everybody's so sweet in Chocolate Town they've forgotten about the strikes in '37 and '53. If you were going to let somebody set up his own country in America, it might as well have been

The worst part of any flood is its aftermath. Any flooding river carries with it ton upon ton of soil—slimy mud when it is wet and microscopic dust when it is dry. The flood that followed Tropical Storm Agnes in 1972 carried devastation from New York to Maryland, but just as bad was the ubiquitous mud it left behind as it receded. (HSDC)

Milton Hershey. The place almost makes you wish your pop had run away with the circus so you could be an orphan. Or it almost makes you look forward to gettin' sick—brand new gorgeous hospital and medical school have been there about six years now. Sort of shaped like a horseshoe. As if this place needed the luck.

June 24, 1972. My third big flood. The mess is horrible, and I'll tell them the smell afterwards is going to be even worse. Somebody said the water will drown 5,000 rats. Baloney. There were never more than 2,000 lobbyists in town at one time.

August 13, 1973. They blew up the Penn Harris Hotel today. There'd have been more fun if they'd have let it burn down the way the old Grand Opera House did on just about the same spot in '09. I'll never forget how excited people used to get about fires, like the Capitol in '97, and the Packing House in '07. Or accidents too, like the Lochiel Train Wreck in '05. Great town for insurance. But where is a fellow going to make a deal now around the Capitol? You can't make a deal in a "motel," even if the place is brand-new and high-priced. If they're to believe what you're promising, you've got to be standing under a high ceiling.

April 15, 1979. At least there's something to smile about in this TMI mess. The kids are wearing some pretty good one-liners on their tee-shirts.

I have that radiant look — I live near TMI.
I survived Three Mile Island — I think.
Gone fission.
Hell no, we won't glow.
I survived the Sooper Dooper Leaker.
We are a nuclear family — we live near TMI.

The Metropolitan Edison people threw one back at them, a tee-shirt that says "Three Mile Island Staff— we stayed behind to save yours." You know what worries me—their insurance isn't that good. That should tell you something. All things considered, you knew what to be afraid of with candles and coal.

June 4, 1981. Well, I'm 105 parties old today. The only one I can't remember is the first one. Probably wasn't much fun for me anyway. Just about everything's changed around here since then. I've seen

The towers of Three Mile Island loom up behind an explanatory panel at the plant's visitor observation tower, located across Route 441 from the facility. The panel gives no explanation for the 1979 accident, however. Courtesy, Mark H. Dorfman

much go down and even more go up—Strawberry Square, all the office buildings and the state buildings, the bridges, all the suburbs and the shopping malls. A boy's not likely anymore to jump school and work in iron and steel the way I did. What would a kid do nowadays at AMP or Berg? Stoke up the computers? And today if your neighborhood's old, you're in luck. Used to mean you were just poor. But the bricks aren't the main thing—a town is people. And I wonder if all the newcomers will be givers or takers. At least two things will stay the same, for sure—straight Harve and that crooked river.

The Harrisburg area suffered financially when Olmstead Air Force Bade closed in the 1960s. Governmental agencies helped find other uses for parts of the former base: the base headquarters, shown here, became the Harrisburg campus of the Pennsylvania State University. The four-year institution now has more than 4,000 students. Courtesy, Pennsylvania State University, Harrisburg."

Harristown has been reshaping the face of downtown Harrisburg since the 1970s. Strawberry Square, the shopping mall, has become the town center of the development. It was designed to attract suburbanites downtown for business again. Courtesy, Harristown Development Corporation

FRONT STREET FROM EXECUTIVE MANSION, HARRISBURG, PA.

When Harve Taylor was young, Front Street was Harrisburg's elite residential street. "Keystone Hall" the Executive Mansion for many years is on the right. Note also the young elm trees on River Front park, planted as part of the City Beautiful Movement. (HSDC)

This photo in 1907 shows Dintaman Boat Yard on the river, although it no longer exists. It was removed when River Front Park was established as part of the City Beautiful Movement which did so much to enhance Harrisburg, thanks to the efforts of leaders like Mira Dock.(HSDC)

The Old State Capitol in Harrisburg, circa 1890, is depicted here in a rare and unique reverse painting on glass. Thin sheets of mother-of-pearl are used for the windows to give a glowing effect. The Capitol, designed by architect Stephen Hills and constructed between 1818 and 1822, was remodeled many times by the time this painting was completed. Courtesy, Private Collection, Woodbourne, New York

The first depiction of the attempted burning of John Harris was painted by William S. Reeder in about 1839. Reeder reputedly consulted with Robert Harris about the event, but his stylistic inspiration comes from Benjamin West's famous painting of William Penn's treaty with the Indians. Reeder's oil painting currently hangs in the governor's mansion. (PHMC)

That Harrisburg was for most of its history a small town set in rich farmland is emphasized in this painting of "Whitehall Farm," done about 1880 by amateur artist Ellen Winebrenner. Note the old capitol at the far right; built to the designs of Stephen Hills between 1818 and 1822, the building burned in 1897. The present Capitol covers its foundations. (HSDC)

In the mid-19th century Charles Magnus depicted this view of Harrisburg from Bridgeport (now Lemoyne). At the center is the Camelback Bridge and to the left is the Cumberland Valley Railroad Bridge. (HSDC)

The Fleming Mansion, now the home of the Harrisburg Civic Club, was the only residence left standing when the River Front Park was created. Behind it stands the old city waterworks. (HSDC)

This novelty postcard provides a conjectural view of mid-19th-century travel in Harrisburg. (PHMC)

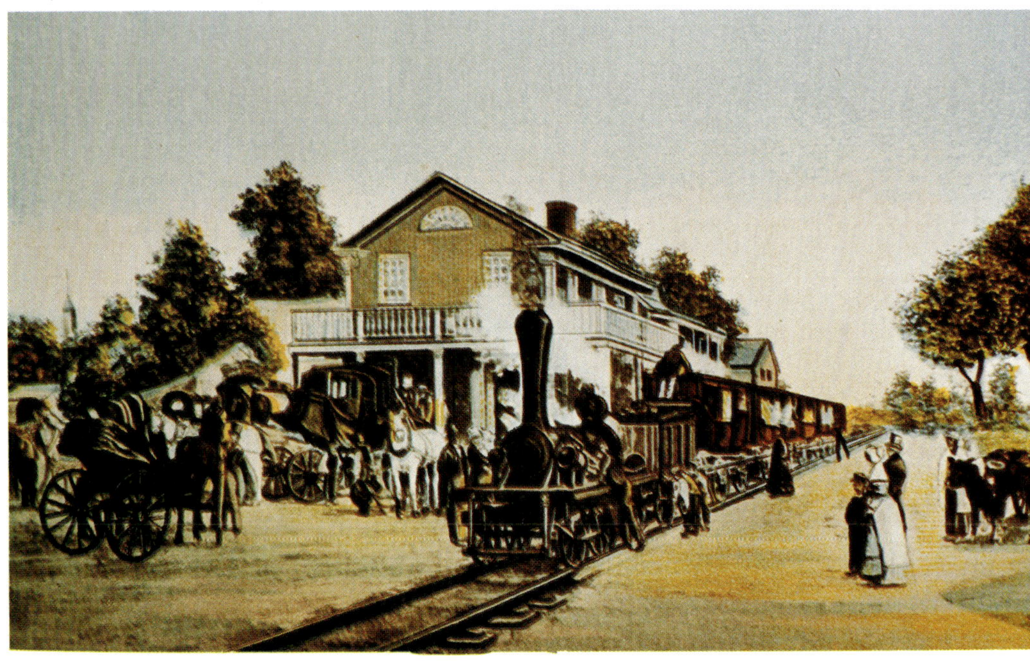

At the turn of the century Market Street was filled with pedestrians, horse-drawn vehicles, and trolley cars. (PHMC)

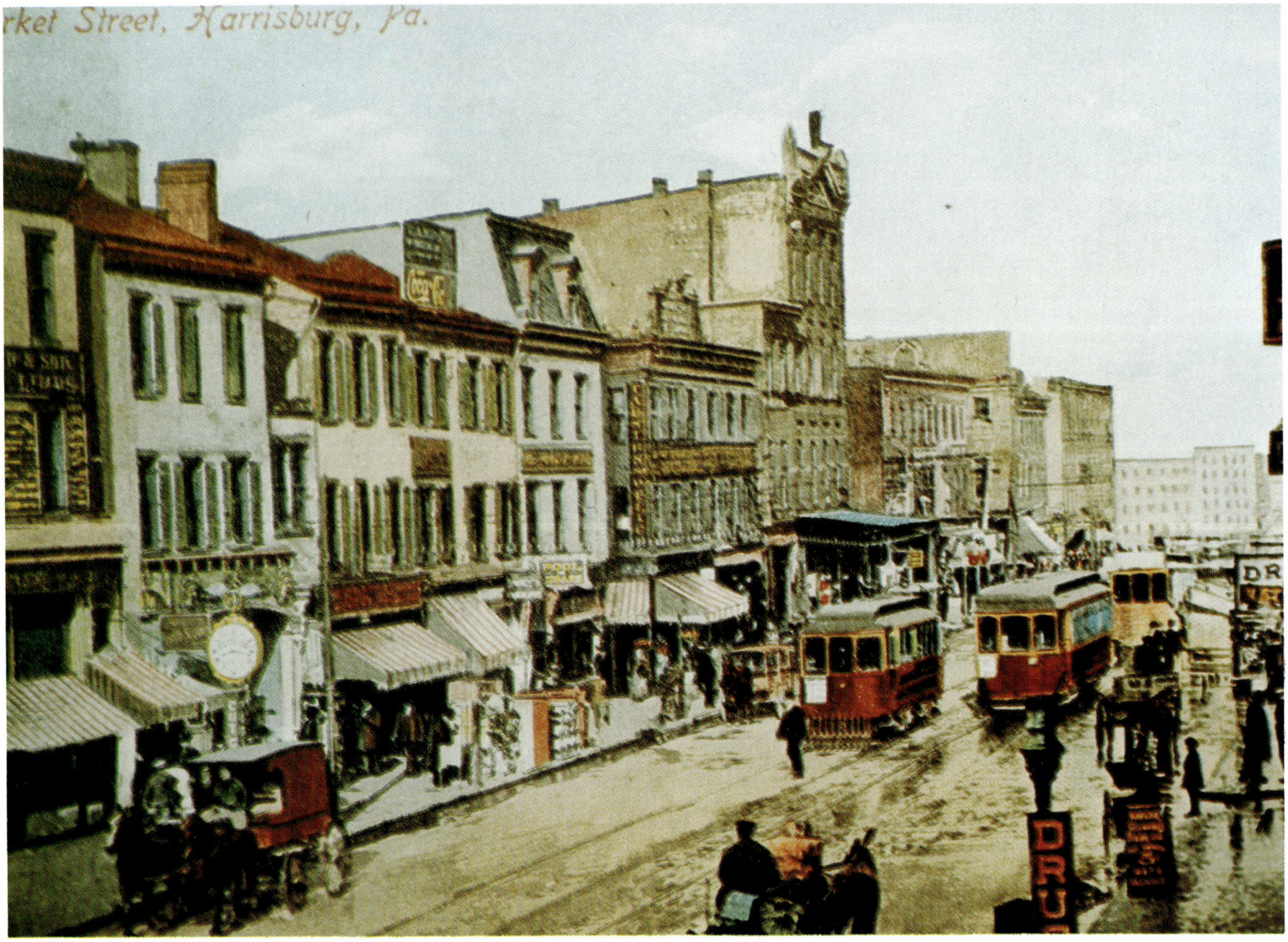

Reservoir Park blooms with children and flowers in this World War I era postcard. (PHMC)

Sadie Hepford and Leonard Sparver married in 1888. The kewpie dolls and the napkin date from their 50th wedding anniversary in 1938. (HSDC) Photo, Mark Dorfman

October 4, 1906, was the date
of the dedication for the new
capitol. Legislators wore these
splendid badges to the
ceremonies where the guest of
honor was President Theodore
Roosevelt. (HSDC)

Harrisburg was an important
manufacturer of blue-
decorated, saltglazed
stoneware. The most famous
potters were Cowden and
Wilcox, makers of the jug on
the right. The water cooler on
the left was made by the less
well known John Young and
Company. It probably belonged
to the Cameron family.
(HSDC)

This early 20th century
postcard shows St. Patrick's
Cathedral on the mall that was
once State Street. (HSDC)

This couple finds spooning in
Paxton Park in 1913 more
attractive than playing tennis.
(PHMC)

The oldest portion of the
Harrisburg City Hospital is
presented in the moonlight in
this early 20th century
postcard. (PHMC)

The Harrisburg Public Library maintains an extensive collection for the use of area residents.

"Greetings from Harrisburg, PA." Harrisburg in the late 1960s. Market Street was still an important, if declining, shopping street. The Capitol was the dominent identifier and the William Penn Memorial Museum and Archives Tower designed by Lawrie and Green were new. Now known as The State Museum of Pennsylvania, the round limestone-clad building was clearly influenced by Frank Lloyd Wright's Guggenheim Museum in New York City. (HSDC)

The present state capitol, completed in 1906, stands on the site of the old one, overlooking the Susquehanna.

The Rockville Bridge, a National Historical Landmark, is the longest stone arch bridge in the world with a length of 3,810 feet.

The Trinity Evangelical
Lutheran Church is a long-
standing house of worship in
Lemoyne.

John Harris built the Harris Mansion in 1766. Later it would be remodeled by Simon Cameron. It now houses the Historical Society of Dauphin County.

Visitors enter the William Penn Museum through the Grand Hall. Inside are the many artifacts and exhibits preserving Pennsylvania history.

The top picture, taken about 1982 from 333 Market Street, the tallest building in the city, shows a bird's eye view of Market Square before its reformation. One sees the modern Commonwealth Bank (far left) at the corner of Market and Front Streets, the new City Government Center (center), and the new Walnut Street Parking garage (far right), but the best is yet to come, shown in the bottom picture, taken by Jeb Stuart in 2007. Now the center of the city has truly tall buildings—the first office building (far left) is the home of M&T Bank (the former Dauphin Deposit bank site) and the Rhoads and Sinon law firm, overshadowing the Dauphin County government offices which have replaced Commonwealth Bank. The Hilton Harrisburg (center), seen from the rear, is commercial Harrisburg's new centerpiece. The odd-shaped complex to the east of the hotel (bottom) is Whitaker Center for Science and the Arts. Across Market Street from the Hilton is the new Penn National Insurance Company headquarters building, and to the north of the Hilton, in front of the parking garage, is another new mixed-use building, Market Square Plaza. Courtesy, Harrisburg City Archives

By the 1980s Harrisburg had an impressive skyline. This view was photographed from a West Shore vantage point that inspired 19th century graphic artists. Photo, Mark Dorfman

The rambling Cameron Mansion was built during the second half of the 19th century for a member of one of the city's wealthiest families. The Italianate-towered house still stands at Front and State Streets where it serves as law offices. (HSDC)

In the top photo, ca. 1982, we have an ordinary stretch of brick storefronts on South Third Street, near Chestnut Street. In the bottom photo, in 2007, the new construction is the International House to the left, built for students and others visiting from abroad. Behind the awnings is the new Bricco Restaurant, managed as part of the culinary training program at the Harrisburg Area Community College. Courtesy, Harrisburg City Archives

The skyline in 2007 is crowded with high-rises, and construction cranes are putting up more. The tallest is 333 Market Street. Courtesy, Harrisburg City Archives

In skyline, ca. 1975, the city has three buildings appearing to match the height of the state capitol dome: the Presbyterian apartments, the Fulton Bank, with its distinctive illuminated letters on the roof, and the City Towers apartments on the far right.

*The Harrisburg Hilton at dusk. The new Post-Modern building provides a
major presence absent since the Penn Harris Hotel was demolished.
Courtesy, City of Harrisburg, Stephen Reed, Mayor*

XV
GREATER HARRISBURG NEIGHBORS

By Mark H. Dorfman

Commerce and industry unite the communities that constitute greater Harrisburg, Pennsylvania's capital area. Geography and history have split it into two distinct regions. Ethnicity and other social forces have fragmented greater Harrisburg into a collection of individual jurisdictions and prevented it from developing into a large, cohesive, powerful urban center.

To the north and east are Derry, Lower Paxton, Susquehanna, and Swatara townships. This sector includes Hershey, Hummelstown, Paxtang, Penbrook, and other communities. To the southeast are Londonderry and Lower Swatara townships, Middletown, Royalton, Highspire, and Steelton—each with its own identity and heritage. Across the river is the West Shore, itself a complex collection of municipalities and neighborhoods.

These are not just bedroom suburbs of Harrisburg. Thousands of state workers do commute daily to the city from the surrounding areas, yet these are distinct communities— each with its own histories and social institutions. Many have their own industries and commercial identities as well. They are part of greater Harrisburg because bridges and highways make travel convenient and because state government is so pervasive an influence. They, like the business and professional firms, industries, associations, and institutions of central Pennsylvania, are Harrisburg's Chronicles of Leadership.

LOWER PAXTON TOWNSHIP

Paxton Township was the American frontier. Settled primarily by Scotch-Irish immigrants in the early 18th century, it was the setting for countless tales of heroism and adventure. When first surveyed in 1729, the township included all of the contemporary Upper Paxton, Middle Paxton, Swatara, and Susquehanna townships as well as the city of Harrisburg.

Paxton Church was founded in 1722. Its services were one of the few touches of civilization in the wilderness. The Scotch-Irish settlers always referred to themselves as God-fearing, peace-loving people. But they were no strangers to fighting. In Scotland, they had rebelled against Britain. In Philadelphia, they feuded with the Quaker government. On the frontier, they warred with the Indians.

Paxton Church, despite the legend on this early 20th century post card, is not the oldest church in Pennsylvania; that honor belongs to Gloria Dei "Old Swedes Church" in Philadelphia. Paxton Church, however, is arguably the oldest church in the capital region. (HSDC)

The Indian Wars produced a source of continuing controversy in Paxton Township. Elsewhere in the country, historians refer to the Paxton Boys with loathing and to their 1763 massacre of the Conestoga Indians as a low point in American history. Nobody questions details about the raid or the follow-up attack at the Lancaster workhouse where surviving Indians had been offered protection by Lancaster County authorities.

But in Paxton Township, the Paxton Boys will always have their defenders. As one local historian wrote in a bicentennial work, "We find our Paxton Rangers much maligned in history books where they are too often depicted as a villainous bunch of cutthroats, rather than the brave, God-fearing, hard-working men they actually were," Lower Paxton is loyal to its own.

MIDDLETOWN

Middletown is the oldest established community in Dauphin County. Named for its location midway from Lancaster to Carlisle, the town was an important stopping-off point on the way west. Through the American Revolution, the town remained the most populous and most important commercial center in the county.

It is a patriotic community. Records of a July 4th celebration held on July 5, 1798, record 15 toasts drunk to various aspects of American life. The celebrants started by drinking "to the anniversary!" and "to the President!"; they ended by drinking "to the arts and sciences!" and "to the fair daughters of America!"

Penn State University architectural historian Irwin Richman likes to point out that Middletown has several restaurants and taverns that have been in continuous use as public houses since the town's days as a stop on the road west and as a terminus of the Union Canal. St. Peters Kirk (church) has been in continuous use as a house of worship since 1767.

On March 28, 1979, Middletown was shaken from its 19th-century complacency by a 20th-century accident. Three Mile Island Nuclear Plant is located just to the south. Early reports of trouble at the plant stunned the community. School closings, rumors, and conflicting reports rapidly added to the confusion. As reporters descended on the community, many residents packed a few precious belongings and evacuated, believing that they might never be able to return. Middletown residents still live with memories of their anger, shock, and fears, as well as uncertainties about long-term effects from the radiation.

Old St. Peters Kirk was founded in 1767 by the patriarch of the Lutheran Church in America, Henry Melchior Muhlenberg, making it the oldest church of its denomination in Dauphin County. In nearby B'nai Jacob, Middletown also houses Dauphin County's oldest Jewish house of worship. Photo by Irwin Richman

STEELTON

Steelton was incorporated in January 1880. But a far more important date in local history is September 22, 1865, the day that the Pennsylvania Steel Company was formed. For Steelton, like Hershey, was a company town.

Two other towns, Baldwin and Ewington, sprung up nearby, but without the support of the company these speculative real estate ventures were short-lived. The company housing was in Steelton, along a stretch of North Front from Locust Alley to Mulberry Street. So too was the company store, located on the river side of the Pennsylvania Canal, facing Locust Street.

The people of Steelton are sturdy and well-tempered. Their bakeries, sausage makers, and other ethnic shops are reminders that Steelton was populated by Eastern European immigrants who came in the closing years of the 19th century. A special census of 1898 listed 33 nationalities in the community.

Like miners, steelworkers learn to live with impending tragedy. Accidents in the plant were common, their cost always high. Local residents learned to live with other forms of disaster as well.

Steelton lies low and close to the river. In 1889, 1902, 1904, 1936, and 1972 destructive floods swept the town. But the most vivid local disaster memory is the Lochiel Train Wreck. On May 11, 1905, the Pennsy's Cleveland Express collided with a freight train carrying dynamite. The toll—22 dead, 130 injured. But Steelton's people always endure— always carry on.

HERSHEY

Derry Township was among the first parts of Dauphin County to attract

white settlers. Derry Church was founded in 1729. Its land patent was signed by sons of William Penn in 1741. But when millions of visitors descend on Derry Township each summer, they do not come to study the distant past but to tour and play in Chocolatetown.

Hershey, Pennsylvania, is not a city, a town, or a village. Only its post office carries the official designation, "Hershey," but the "town square" of this community in Derry Township is formed by the intersection of Chocolate and Cocoa avenues. The street lights are shaped like chocolate kisses. On many days, the sweet

The center of Steelton was prosperous and booming in the early 20th century. The trolley car connected the industrial city with Harrisburg as well as with many smaller nearby communities. (HSDC)

Hershey was a company town ruled by a mostly benevolent patriarch in Milton S. Hershey. The railway station was placed at the center of town, next to the chocolate factory. Early in the 20th century, Mr. Hershey also provided decent, supervised living quarters for some of his employees. (HSDC)

aroma of cocoa fills the air. Official or not, this is Hershey.

The history of Hershey, Pennsylvania, is the history of Hershey Chocolate. Like Steelton, Hershey was a company town—built along with the factory to house and support the workers. And while the firm provided a street railroad from Hummelstown to Campbelltown, Hershey has remained the center of the world for generations of central Pennsylvania workers.

Milton S. Hershey, founder of the chocolate company, was born in 1857 near Hockersville in Derry Township. In 1900 he sold his Lancaster Caramel Company, manufacturer of "Crystal A" caramels and other popular sweets, for one million dollars. But he reserved the right to keep making chocolate candy.

On January 28, 1903, a corps of surveyors arrived in Derry Township to begin surveying for a factory, streets, houses, water mains, sewage system, trolley lines, and a park. Hershey had decided to build not only a new chocolate factory, but a town to go with it.

The impressive public buildings of Hershey, its community center (now executive offices for Hershey Foods), Hotel Hershey, the high school, and the sports arena were all built by the company during the Great Depression—in part to keep local construction workers employed, in part because the cost of building materials was very low. For the rest of his life Milton Hershey remained proud that "no man... was dropped by reason of the Depression. And no salaries were cut."

All has not always been idyllic in Chocolatetown. There have been strikes and ethnic conflict, even during the lifetime of the founder. In recent years, the transformation of the chocolate company to a complex modern corporation has altered the relationship between the town and the firm—residents have taken more responsibility for their own political and economic affairs.

HUMMELSTOWN

Founded around 1740, Hummelstown is one of the older communities in Derry Township. A small, quiet, primarily agricultural community between Harrisburg and Hershey, Hummelstown became the focus of national attention late in 1955 when one of its residents defied the right of the United States government to tell her how to run her farm.

Elsie Mumma was charged in September 1955 with overplanting her wheat acreage quota by 18 acres. The government assessed $403.20 in fines and penalties; she decided to fight. The image of this lone farmer standing her ground against the government will always be remembered as former *Patriot* writer Bern Sharfman told it.

The Mumma family came to the United States in 1624. Elsie

Hummelstown, shown in this mid 20th century post card typifies the settled small towns of our region. The view of homes and churches is little changed today, (HSDC)

Mumma was graduated in 1922 with the first coeducational class at Gettysburg College. She later learned to fly airplanes, danced with Bill (Bojangles) Robinson, and performed at Madison Square Garden with Barbara Hutton. Pictures of her appeared in Vogue and *New Yorker* magazines. She became the first woman to join the National Association of Life Underwriters' Million Dollar Round Table.

When her father died in 1948, Elsie Mumma promised him that she would maintain the farm. She came home to keep the promise. And when the government tried to enforce crop controls, she rebelled. "As long as I own the land, pay my taxes, pay my debts, and ask for no aid, the land is mine... to protect, to plant, to harvest." Hummelstown agreed.

THE WEST SHORE
West Shore real estate is among the most valuable in central Pennsylvania. From a historian's viewpoint that is surprising, because for many years almost nobody wanted it.

Today the West Shore consists of a large and diverse group of municipalities: Camp Hill, Lemoyne, New Cumberland, Mechanicsburg, Shiremanstown, Wormleysburg, West Fairview, Enola, Marysville, Hampden Township, East Pennsboro Township, Lower Allen Township, Fairview Township, and other communities. Yet under early plans for the region, much of this land—the core area between the Yellow Breeches and the Conodoguinet creeks, from St. Johns Road to the River—was a single unit known to the Penn family as Louther Manor.

Archaeological evidence and historic records suggest that local Native American tribes were only passively interested in West Shore lands. The Susquehannock (Conestoga) Indians set up a few camps

The rapid suburbanization of the West Shore has often obscured the region's rural past as typified by the no longer standing Orr's Bridge, that crossed the Conodoguinet Creek near Camp Hill. (HSDC)

Harrisburg Airport in New Cumberland (now Capital City Airport) was the first major commercial airport serving Harrisburg. The Art Deco buildings and the latest TWA plane demonstrated that the region was proud of its status in this newest field of transportation (HSDC)

in the area as early as 1616. The Iroquois Nation conquered the area around 1675. And the Lenape (Delawares) were resettled there by the Iroquois toward the end of the century.

The Penn family offered to sell the lands from Silver Spring to the river to John Harris, Sr. But Harris was pleased with his more valuable East Shore location, and found the price of 5,000 pounds (about 50 cents an acre) excessive. The Penns then offered it to the Shawnee in an attempt to get them out of Paxton Township. But, perhaps because they had already been granted privileges in the area by the Iroquois, the Shawnee rejected the Penns' offer.

Despite the refusal of the Shawnee to accept their offer, the Penns tried to prevent white settlement in the area. This may have been a prudent attempt to use the West Shore as a buffer zone between the German settlers of York County to the south and the Ulstermen to the north (Perry County) and east (Paxton Township).

Louther Manor had been explored and surveyed for the Penn family by Peter Chartier, a son of French pioneer Martin Chartier and his Indian wife. Peter Chartier was an exception to the Penns' "no white settlement" policy; he was granted title to lands in Louther Manor between the

Yellow Breeches and what is now 16th Street, New Cumberland.

The second exception (and first permanent structure) was William Kelso's Tavern, opened in 1734. The tavern became a West Shore terminal for the ferry John Harris had begun operating one year earlier.

But the land remained largely unoccupied, what West Shore historian Robert Crist has described as "an island in a sea of settlement." It was not until 1770 that the Penns started granting patents from Louther Manor. Only in 1771 did Robert Whitehill construct the area's first stone building, his house at what is now 19th and Market streets in Camp Hill.

Shortly thereafter, some settlement formed along the roads through the region, especially along the road from the "lower crossing" (used by westbound traffic), Simpson's Ferry. Eastbound traffic used the "upper crossing" at Harris' Ferry. Later, those who could afford the toll used the Camelback Bridge from Harrisburg to Bridgeport (now Lemoyne). The area near Trindle Springs along the Simpson Ferry Road became known as Mechanicsburg in recognition of its wagon builders, wheelwrights, and repair shops.

The Civil War's Gettysburg campaign produced some anxious moments for Harrisburg, and some actual confrontations around the West Shore's Bridgeport and Oyster Point. Mechanicsburg was actually occupied by the Confederacy for four days. It was not the town's finest hour. As local historian Norman Keefer describes events, local leaders took down the town flag and surrendered it to the rebels when threatened with a destructive search. And "farmers' wives baked themselves into a state of exhaustion to supply bread and cake for the invaders."

The war was just one in a long series of reverses for West Shore inventor Daniel Drawbaugh, whose Eberly Mills birthplace is identified by a state historic marker. According to biographer Warren Harder, Drawbaugh was born poor and died poor, but his life was a remarkable series of "almosts" and "potential." He came within a controversial 4-3 vote of the U.S. Supreme Court of being recognized as the inventor of the telephone. He was a major stockholder in the company that "almost" replaced American Bell. Drawbaugh later invented a wireless voice transmitter (it sent signals through ground and water) that, "almost" replaced Marconi's radio.

Historic markers also denote the location of Fort Couch at Eighth and Ohio streets in Lemoyne. The breastworks there were thrown up to resist the expected Confederate advance during the Gettysburg campaign. According to the marker, "a few Confederate scouts neared here but withdrew." A marker on State Highway 641 just west of Camp Hill identifies Peace Church. The 1798 stone church, one of the oldest in Cumberland County, is near the site of an old Indian graveyard.

A lasting tribute to those who passed through the Harrisburg area on their way to build new lives is the brief, understated historic marker on Simpson Street near Walnut Street in Mechanicsburg. It marks the Simpson Ferry Road "Built about 1792. It extended from Michael Simpson's Ferry on the Susquehanna to Carlisle.... Used by many persons traveling to western part of State." And to a new world.

The Penn Harris Hotel was the city's first metropolitan hotel which Harrisburgers compared favorably to New York's Waldorf Astoria. Its restaurants and ballrooms made it a center of the city's political and social life. It was the model for "The Fort Penn Hotel" in John O'Hara sensational *roman á clef* about Harrisburg, *A Rage to Live*. Torn down when it was judged obsolete, the site is occupied by Strawberry Square. (HSDC)

XVI
LIFE BY THE OVERFLOWING ROAD

A "People's Bridge" sounds vaguely communistic to me, like it's not actually mine, no matter what they say, and they're going to make me use it, even if I'd rather stay on my own side. But the People's Bridge we're talking about here—the Walnut Street Bridge, Old Shaky—was the real thing, built by an American capitalist who gave the people what they wanted.

Elias Zollinger Wallower was the sort of man who would put up a bridge if he had a mind to. He was born in 1854, the son of a railroad agent and local politician. He attended the Harrisburg Academy, learned shorthand, and became a reporter, covering both the Centennial *in Philadelphia and the Molly Maquires' trial in 1876. At age 22 he became the publisher of the first penny newspaper in town, the* Daily Independent. *Later he was president of the Harrisburg Light, Heat, and Power Company; president of the Mt. Holly Brick and Clay Company; and vice-president of the Harrisburg Pipe and Pipe Bending Company. He also helped start the Harrisburg Steam Heat Company and helped build the YMCA and the Harrisburg Country Club. He was proudest, he said, of building the Penn-Harris Hotel. Like so many of Harrisburg's late nineteenth leaders, his profits came directly from industrial progress. Famed columnist Paul Beers said of Wallower, in the* Evening News *on July 23, 1976, "he accomplished inestimable good by being the go-getter that he was."*

In his wonderfully readable Reminiscences, *published privately in 1941 (the same year he died), Mr. Wallower recalled building his bridge. "The tolls charged by the Market Street bridge, a complete monopoly, were exorbitant," he wrote. This capitalist knew a ripple effect when he saw one: the Harrisburg Bridge Company's Market Street Bridge tolls "prevented free access to the city," they were "a detriment to merchants," and they were a "cause of high prices for market produce." Wallower had personal objections too:*

"It cost me 45 cents, or 90 cents for the round trip, each time I drove to my country home at Mechanicsburg, with my two-horse conveyance. I am strongly under the impression that this fact had much to do with the building of the new bridge."

He canvassed for subscriptions around Cumberland County, especially among the farmers, who were not very helpful, but finally he was successful. He and his People's Bridge Company investors contracted with a builder, the Phoenix Bridge Company, to put up a prefabricated, light-weight, wrought-iron truss bridge for $200,000. Before construction was started, however, Wallower asked the president of the Harrisburg Bridge Company if he couldn't just buy the offending structure. The president told him no, Wallower couldn't buy it. Wallower said the president was later heard to say that "Young Wallower might as well try to build a bridge to the moon." This jibe, said Wallower, "did not have the effect desired, of lessening my inten-

tion." Always diplomatic, he didn't mention the president's name. In fact, the 35-year-old Wallower was up against the city's First Families: the Harrisburg Bridge Company had been started by the McCormicks, the Camerons, and the Haldemans, and was still controlled by them.

They continued to fight Wallower, trying to stop him by complaining to the state Attorney General that his bridge piers would obstruct navigation on the Susquehanna. The Attorney General granted a writ against Wallower, but that was overturned in court, ending that "humorous" episode of obstruction, as Wallower put it. In retaliation, his engineers brought out a report that questioned the structural integrity of the Market Street Bridge. The Harrisburg Bridge Company then tried to stop him from putting his bridge across City Island. Wallower's builder, Dean and Westbrook, defied that effort by buying the entire island. That was the end of the man-made opposition.

The flood of 1889 crested at 26.8 feet, highest on record, more than 9 feet over flood stage, and that persuaded the builders to make the piers six feet higher—thank goodness, or the bridge might not have made it past 1894, when a flood crested at 25.7 feet, the second worst flood to that date. The People's Bridge was completed in 1889 and officially opened in 1890. Some record-keeper noted that Mr. John Probst was the first person to pay his toll and cross, on Saturday morning, April 26, at five minutes past one o'clock.

The charter promised that the People's Bridge tolls would not exceed ten cents for a "one horse and

Elias Z. Wallower was the dynamic businessman who built the Walnut Street bridge as well as the Penn Harris Hotel. (HSDC)

The Walnut Street bridge is the backdrop for a boat race on the Susquehanna around the turn of the 20th century. Spectators stand on the bridge and along the rough unimproved shoreline before the development of River Front Park. (HSDC)

four wheeled vehicle and driver" (there were sixteen different tolls, depending on what you were bringing across). Not surprisingly, "our bridge received all of the patronage," said Wallower. That started a price war. The Market Street bridge lowered its standard toll to five cents so the farmers switched back to that route. Wallower then lowered his to five cents and sat tight. The two companies then reached a truce: Wallower would charge ten cents, Market Street would charge fifteen cents, and they would divide all revenue equally. When the agreement expired, both bridges charged ten cents to cross. The state purchased the Market Street Bridge in 1949 and abolished tolls in 1957. The Pennsylvania Department of Transportation eventually owned Wallower's bridge too, which came to be known as the Walnut Street Bridge and, unofficially, "Old Shaky." On June 5, 1972, it was named to the National Register of Historic Places.

The terrible flood that year was hard on the bridge but didn't break

it. Repairs were made, and it reopened in 1974, if only to pedestrian traffic. It was in this weakened condition that citizens became most strongly attached to it. Now you could safely linger on it, and see how funny it felt to walk on the iron grid deck (cars used to "sing" when they rode on the grid), and you could lean on the railing and watch the fireworks, or the ice break. Joggers and cyclists were dependent on it, and fans walking to baseball games on the Island were indebted to it. Old Shaky amiably joined the suburbs to the city. Here was the happiest spot on the prettiest waterfront you ever saw. The other bridges—South, Market Street, and Harvey Taylor— carry much more traffic, of course, but they don't lift as many hearts as this one does.

With its history in mind, we can better understand the enormous attention that was paid to the bridge's partial destruction in the flood of January, 1996. The way it happened was quite sensational; the way we handled it was rather sentimental.

The Walnut Street bridge survived various floods. In 1936 parts of it were submerged. Harrisburg's major skyscraper in 1936 was the Harrisburger Hotel which is clearly visible in the view of Harrisburg from the West Shore. (HSDC)

It was the two worst weeks in the city's history, said Mayor Stephen Reed. The travail started on January 7, with 20 inches of snow. Eleven more inches came down on January 12. The total for the month was now 39 inches, a record. Suddenly the temperature shot up: the high was 42 degrees on January 14, 43 on the 15th, and 56 on the 19th. In addition to the melt, nearly 1 inch of rain fell in the city, 3 inches in the upper Susquehanna basin. That day the frozen river's ice broke up and then jammed up, stalling the river's flow. The Susquehanna was 7 feet high at 5:00 p.m. on January 19; by 9:30 p.m. it was 20 feet high, the fastest rise ever recorded. Twenty-six neighborhoods were evacuated that night and the next day, moving about 8,000 persons in all.

On January 20th, while crowds of people were watching the overflowing river, the city had its most dramatic modern disaster. At 2:30 in the afternoon, part of the western half of the Walnut Street bridge suddenly gave way. Two iron spans started floating down the ice-filled river, heading toward the Market Street bridge. Spectators gasped and cameras clicked. Five people were standing on the Walnut Street Bridge when it gave way; luckily, they were in the right place, on the part that stayed put. "God was with us," said Pete Magaro, the last man to cross. Within seconds Old Shaky smashed into its former competitor, and fell to pieces like a toy being stepped on. The massive, concrete Market Street Bridge didn't budge, and Shaky's remains disappeared into the water and under the bridge. It was one for the books.

The Shipoke neighborhood was flooded as usual, not only with water but with slabs of ice the size of cars. Then, early on the morning of January 22, more destruction was visited upon it. At 104 Conoy Street, faulty wiring from an electrical panel box (which had nothing to do with the flooding) started a fire that spread rapidly throughout Pancake Row, a picture-postcard (literally) set of eight refurbished row houses on Conoy Street that had been built in 1890, the same time as the Walnut Street Bridge. Three workers at Pennsy Supply Company a few blocks away saw the smoke and turned in an alarm to the fire department. Then, thinking quickly, they drove two large, front-end loaders down to Shipoke to help clear the ice slabs out of the way for the fire trucks. More than a hundred firefighters were called in to battle the four-alarm blaze; they had to work in hip-deep, freezing water and try to keep from falling down on the ice. Fire equipment was damaged and men were nearly frozen, but after three and a half hours the fire was put out. If they hadn't reached Pancake Row in time, said Mayor Reed, if the Pennsy men— Alan Deiter, John Paul, and Jim Wolfgang—hadn't led the way with their loaders, the whole neighborhood might have burned down. Fire Chief Donald Konkle congratulated the Pennsy men too, saying it would have been easy for them to have turned their backs after they had turned in the alarm. But John Paul humbly told a reporter, "We were in loaders, we had heaters, and it was dry. I saw firefighters wading in it and falling in it, but not stopping."

City Island at sunset. The river shimmers and a baseball game is in progress in the stadium on City Island. Taken before the disastrous flood that damaged it, the intact Walnut Street Bridge connects both the East and West Shores with City Island. Courtesy, City of Harrisburg, Stephen Reed, Mayor

Above and on pages 159 and 160, the Walnut Street bridge is being swept downstream on January 20, during the "Flood of '96." These compelling photos showing the structure's gradual destruction were taken by William Fasnacht, a riverfront resident of Cumberland Road in Lemoyne. (HSDC)

As if the Fates wanted to make sure the winter was memorable, on February 6, a second fire struck Shipoke just around the corner from the first one at Pancake Row. Houses at 561 and 563 South Front—the ones firefighters had saved two weeks before—were badly damaged. "It's almost surreal," said the Mayor.

Historians will find ample documentation of the complete disaster. Teresa Copenhaver happened to be in Negley Park with her video camera; she shot the bridge's destruction and gave the video to Channel 27, who gave her $27.

From there it made its way to ABC, the Weather Channel, CNN, and the entire world. From his home in Lemoyne on the west shore, Bill Fasnacht took a series of still photos of the bridge breaking loose and going down; he gave his negatives to the Historical Society of Dauphin County. The Shipoke flooding and fire were well-covered too—television had impressive footage of aerial trucks, belching smoke, and the incredible amount of crud that had piled up, while newspapers carried human interest stories about victims who also happened to be good interviewees. Reporters said the damage to Pancake Row was estimated at one million dollars, an appraisal that the Row's owners may not have wanted the county's tax assessor to hear. The *Patriot-News* published a special section on February 8th that provided a retrospective on the disaster and editorialized on the bravery and endurance of both the survivors and their rescuers. "When nature was at its worst, they were humanity at its best," proclaimed the paper. Three months later, on April 15, WHP-TV broadcast its own titanic production, "The People's Bridge," featuring U.S. House Speaker Newt Gingrich's memories of crossing the bridge when he was growing up here. Old-timers might have thought all this solemnization was a little corny—but still a perfectly true account.

The aftermath of these disasters shows how quickly Americans can clean up a mess and even take advantage of it. Within a month, the Structural Technical Group of the Central Pennsylvania Section of the American Society of Civil Engineers was holding a conference about the

Walnut Street Bridge, featuring engineer speakers from the Department of Transportation, the City of Harrisburg, and Penn State's Department of Architectural Engineering. Wisely, they scheduled a social hour with cash bar before the lectures started. Spirited citizens, led by the Historic Harrisburg Association and the Pennsylvania Historical and Museum Commission, immediately announced the formation of the People's Bridge Preservation Campaign. Now the bridge was meaningful because it was, unsentimentally, "the primary pedestrian link to a revitalized City Island regional recreation complex," said one of their posters. By May the People's Bridge Coalition was formed, supported by more than fifty organizations and a thousand members, including " Descendants of E. Z. Wallower," said their newsletter, *The Phoenix*.

To raise money for the Walnut Street Bridge/Waterfront Trust Fund, hundreds of pieces from the true bridge were sold—small sections of pipe-shaped iron truss you could use as a paperweight or blunt instrument—as well as commemorative bridge videotapes and T-shirts, all this enterprise producing more than $55,000. Unfortunately, the first two sales had dealt in bridge pieces that contained lead paint. The final sale would offer only relics that had been "soaked in a cleaning solution and scrubbed, then covered in a coat of clear acrylic," said the city, ever-mindful of its liability. If desired, one could exchange, at no extra charge, a previously purchased leaded relic for an unleaded one. The Mayor remarked that he was "amazed" at the support for the bridge.

By August of 1996 repairs to the

piers of the Harrisburg side of the Walnut Street Bridge were well underway. Workers had discovered that the piers were not built of blocks of stone throughout; instead, the interiors had simply been filled with slag, and that was probably why the piers had weakened. The new ones were made of poured cement, molded and colored to make them look like the originals. Repairs to the eastern half cost $6 million.

PennDOT invited public discussion on how to fix the western half of the bridge, from restoring the bridge exactly, to substituting modern spans, to building a whole new bridge, to "Do-Nothing." The Coalition hoped for a design that would be "functional and attractive without being extravagant," which sounds like the American Dream in general. On April 16, 1998, PennDOT announced its intentions: the western half of the bridge would be restored with "look-alike" spans using modern materials. There was no need to offer several options, added PennDOT, because three-quarters of the people they asked wanted some kind of restoration, not a new contraption. PennDOT expects a look-alike version to cost $10.78 million; restoring the spans "in historical context" would cost $11.8 million. Look-alike is "not a perfect solution," said Randy King, the Mayor's spokesman, but it returns the bridge to service, "and that's what's important in the long run." In the summer of 1998 Old Shaky was officially dubbed a National Historic Civil Engineering Landmark. It is "a great example of bridge construction techiques used more than a hun-

dred years ago," said Brian McCoola, president of the local chapter of the American Society of Civil Engineers. "The Phoenix-truss system is distinctive, and only a handful exist to remind us of our past."

Shipoke was almost all put back together by the fall 1997. The five-houses in Pancake Row that were still standing after the fire had been repaired and improved and the residents were returned; the three addresses that had to be rebuilt from scratch were to be finished around Christmastime. On October 12, the neighborhood had a party across the street in Riverfront Park. About 400 celebrants attended, many of them wearing "Shipoke—Venice on the Susquehanna" T-shirts (last winter it looked more like Sarajevo, said Beth Balaban). The neighborhood formally thanked everyone, from the ladies of the Red Cross, whose mobile kitchen fed everyone during the cleanup, to the yellow-uniformed inmates of Dauphin County Prison, who pitched in by shoveling lots of muck into trucks. The three saviours from Pennsy Supply were applauded again and given presents, and again the men insisted that the real heroes were the firefighters. Officials declared that Shipoke's rescue and recovery were made possible by outstanding community spirit, private and public leadership, and effective municipal services. I'll drink to that, but, speaking as a landlord of Pancake Row, I have to say that something else kept us afloat this time, something that was usually missing here after the floods of 1936 and 1972: a helluva lot of insurance.

LEVEL
CAFÉ FRESCO
BREAKFAST • LUNCH • DINNER • COCKTAILS
CAFÉ FRESCO

XVII
JANUARY 28, 1998: THE ACTION STARTS ON SECOND

At one time, Harrisburg's most famous avenue was Front Street, the main thoroughfare running alongside the Susquehanna River. Postcards pictured the city's spacious first street, its variety of mansions, and its skyline of occasional skyscrapers. Today, Front Street still looks good, but the action is along Second Street, the main drag that gives commuters and visitors access to and through the city. The busiest blocks on Second Street, from Market to North Streets, are now known as Restaurant Row. There have been eateries and watering holes in this section of Second Street since the city was founded, but now their presence would appear to be the avenue's main purpose.

A search of the *Patriot-News* online archives reveals that the phrase "Restaurant Row" was first used on January 28, 1998, when the Fire House restaurant took over the site at 606 North Second that was previously occupied by the Hope Station restaurant, and before that, Jimmy's Firehouse. Originally, the building was the home of the Hope Engine Company No. 2, constructed in 1871. Reporter Sue Gleiter wrote that new owner Don Brown "liked to think Second Street will do for Harrisburg what Fell's Point has achieved in Baltimore or Restaurant Row has accomplished in Philadelphia." He said, "I just think this downtown offers the potential" that "people don't realize." Brown was a prescient leader of what would be the Row.

Later, on August 9, 1998, the newspaper was headlining "Downtown Develops as a Hub of Hospitality." The lynchpin of the hub was the new Hilton Harrisburg Hotel. Brown was interviewed again, saying "The whole downtown is picking up. The Hilton started it, and it's gotten better from there." Reporter Gleiter wrote, "It is now hip to stick around Harrisburg after work." Pat Carroll, in an accompanying story, asserted that "with the Hilton, for once, Harrisburg didn't get a bush-league substitute. We got the nice lobby with dark Pennsylvania cherry on the walls, Steve Rudolph at the piano, and a restaurant [the four-diamond Golden Sheaf] classy enough to impress a visiting in-law." The new hotel was one of Hilton's two "Concierge Class" properties in Pennsylvania, with manager Bill Kohl already selling 10,000 rooms a month and writing four million dollars in local paychecks every four weeks. K.J. and Stephen Weinstock's metropolitan-style "Stock's on Second," the second hit restaurant to open in February '98, was attracting a mix of Generation X and baby-boomer professionals, demonstrating that downtown revitalization was a sociological as well as a political, financial and architectural phenomenon. However, old-time Second Street restaurateurs Jimmy Kaldes (The Spot) and George N. Gekas (The Gazebo Room) offered an historical perspective on the new developments. "We had slow days, but it got better. I was not nervous," said Kaldes. "I've seen this town in the good days and the bad days," said Gekas.

The names of Second Street's restaurants, bars, lounges, pubs, and clubs are definitely not etched in stone or welded in place, but here are the establishments a hungry investigator would find operating in early 2009.

The Row starts at the Hilton Harrisburg, on the northeast corner of Market Square, showing off

St. Patrick's Day turns into night and the beat goes on.

the most formal restaurant downtown, the Golden Sheaf. The hotel also has more informal facilities (Raspberries) and a bar with jazz outside in the summer. Hilton's the class action on Second.

If you cross Second street (with the light), heading westward toward the Martin Luther King, Jr., City Government Center (still known informally as "city hall"), then turn north, you first encounter Club Privado. There have been many mini-bars by other names in this space (including an oxygen bar), which takes up the narrow first floor of what was Harrisburg's first skyscraper, the Union Trust building.

North of Privado are the offices of the Harrisburg Downtown Improvement District, the official facilitator for the Second street improvements, first headed by controversial Fred Clark. He wanted to get the hot dog vendors off the street corners and the buses out of Market Square, in order to foster a European ethos in the 'Burg. Jeff Murison is in charge now. It's the DID that put up the 250 hanging flower baskets downtown, paid for with extra taxes placed on the Row's property owners.

Continue northward, past the Charles Schwab brokerage, cross Walnut Street, and you see on the corner the remains of The Spot, but more about that later. Next is Palumbo's Italian Eatery, then the Chinese New 2nd Wok, and then Zia's at the Red Door, a wine bar auxiliary to the larger Zia's Trattoria restaurant. Next to Zia's is Brinjac Engineering and the new Pennsylvania State Bank, but there used to be an Italian restaurant there (Cantone's Downtown), and prior to that a rendezvous loosely French (Politesse), proving the Row can change quickly. Cross Locust Street, pass Cobalt Hair Salon and the Psychic's shop, and you come to the stainless steel mobile diner that was hauled there in 2006 and will soon be hauled away to make room for a new 18-story office building. Originally known as Tom Sawyer's, the diner was changed to Sawyer's Cantina, an association that would puzzle Mark Twain. Up from the Cantina and its adjoining party yard and bandstand is a long-time empty travel office, then 2nd Street Pizza, and then Zembie's, a bar and café that was operating before the beginning of the Second Street experience. Next to Zembie's are the dance and music clubs that give Second Street its rowdy reputation—the Dragonfly Club, and the Hardware Bar and Eclipse Night Club. This is where the crowds gather and where the action is youngest and loudest.

Indeed, the relative mayhem, noise and trash on this corner became a problem in 2002, when the Row was first rip-roaring. The city "now must deal with the hangover," wrote reporter. John Luciew on May 10th. The Row needed more police, more parking, and more public toilets. One August night in '02, police and fire fighters evacuated 1,165 patrons from the clubs because they exceeded their limit of 373. On August 24, 2002, a *Patriot-News* editorial writer ("Let it Be") showed his age when he colorfully groused about some of the changes taking place downtown. Harrisburg used to be a city,

he said, "where beer tasted like beer and not like gooseberries with a hint of cinnamon, and was sloshed up in establishments with names like Peanut Joe's, the K Bar, the Clock Bar, the Senate Horseshoe Bar, the Little Ritz, the Esquire and the Warner . . . . Dinner menu?   T-bone steaks, "french or mashed," pork chops, roast beef with brown gravy, salmon cakes, fried chicken—simple stuff. Coffee came out of an urn rather than from some hellish device that spits and hisses like a steam engine fighting for headway. . . .maybe it wasn't New York City-grade, but nothing to be ashamed of . . .Improve and burnish the downtown image, but don't neglect the city's roots."

One suspects that the young revelers paid no attention to the old fogey, perhaps mainly for the reason that they don't read newspapers.

Four months later, in December, 2002, an argument that started in the Dragonfly club ended in a gun killing in a downtown garage, but that didn't scare

The Brick Haus is getting ready for St. Pat's too, although the ambience is German.

Spice shows off its fare to the street. The restaurant used to be Fisaga.

The space occupied by Sawyer's Cantina and its bandstand area is scheduled to be taken by another skyscraper.

away the crowds. "It's not like the area is a war zone or something," said one customer. On the other hand, a downtown resident complained to the newspaper that row "can be pronounced 'rou,' a word that means an uproar, a brawl. Is that what Restaurant Row has become?" Police Capt. Isaac Nixon told reporter John Luciew on August 8, 2004, "We have two to three fights a night. Guys get their beer muscles. . . . It's not that bad down there. My biggest worry is somebody getting run over by a car. They won't cross at the crosswalks." There was a second deadly fight at Second and Cranberry in 2006, as the clubs and bars were emptying, but that did not kill the Row either.

One ironic development is that Greater Harrisburg residents appear to have become a minority percentage of the downtown crowd. Ron Kamionka, developer of five bars including Eclipse and Hardware, can tell by tracking the computerized ID swipes that only one-third of the crowd is from the immediate east and west shore suburbs. "On Friday and Saturday nights, it's a destination point. . . . we don't realize how big of an animal we have created," he told Luciew in an August, 2004 interview. Whatever the case, the *Patriot-News* keeps reporting, and thus promoting, every new development on the Row. A search of its online archive reveals almost 400 mentions of "Restaurant Row" from 1998 to 2008.

But let us continue the tour up the west side of Second Street. Across Pine Street, on the corner, there's a building being re-developed that used to be a KoKoMo's Sports Bar and Grill, and before that, a traditional Greek restaurant, the Colonnade. Farther up Second, past what used to be Hillary Clinton's presidential campaign headquarters, is Ceoltas Irish Pub, a busy new restaurant and bar. Next to Ceoltas used to be Javid's Indian Grill and Hooka Lounge, which took the place of a small, traditional Italian restaurant; for now, the space is empty. Next comes He She Hair and the old State Café, and towering over that is the high-rise Presbyterian Apartments building. Who knows how their residents take to the partying below?

Continuing north on Second Street and crossing South Street, you now come to Egypt, a dark martini lounge that used to be called Mars. Co-owner of is Rick Galiardo, night spot developer on the Row. After Eygpt, the bars and restaurants disappear until you cross State Street, then Liberty Street, and come to the Fire House Restaurant, the spark that helped start everything. North of the Fire House is the last eatery on Second Street, the 2nd Street Kabob, one of the latest entries and another ethnic effort.

That sums up the west side of Restaurant Row, running from Market to North Street. If you don't come across the same names today when you walk up the Row, then treat this description like the details in an old photograph and be impressed with the quickness of capitalism's dynamism. The economist Joseph Schumpeter was not being unnecessarily cruel in calling an evolutionary process like Restaurant Row "creative destruction."

Now, if you walk down the east side of Second Street back toward the Hilton, you meet the rest of the action. The hole in the ground at Second and State Streets is the foundation for a chic 13-story hotel that will go up. The Starwood Aloft is being developed by dot.com millionaire J. Alex Hartzler, president of WCI Partners, a new player in the city. The partner who joined him in September, 2008, is Hasu Shah, another ambitious entrepreneur. Starwood Aloft will have a pool

and alfresco dining, the new symbol of culinary cool. A block east of Aloft, close to the Capitol, will be the 10-story Cosmopolitan Hotel. Next stop on the Row, coming after the former Barak Obama presidential campaign headquarters, is The Quarter, across the street from Ceoltas. The Quarter's theme is New Orleans-style food and drink, presented in a new two-story bar and restaurant that transformed the space once belonging to a house of worship. Making your way down the rest of the block, you pass the high-rise Verizon headquarters, then cross Pine Street and Sovereign Bank to the core of the Row again. Tightly packed together are the German-American Cragin's Brick Haus; the Miyako Sushi on Second; an empty card and gift shop; a True Value hardware store that used to be across the street where the night clubs are now; another empty shop; a tobacco shop; and the Art House Lounge, a small art gallery. Business picks up at the Café Fresco-Center City, which has a new lounge, Level 2, on the second floor, and then you walk around the sidewalk tables at Stock's on Second, one of the larger restaurants that helped start the Row.

The only place where you can eat bison on Second Street is the Neato Burrito, a proudly funky joint south of Stock's. Down from the Burrito is Spice (formerly Fisaga), which is ground zero of the Row, the corner of Second and Locust Streets. Spice has tables on the sidewalk too, announcing that this is the Row, and here are the people. Alfresco dining at Spice is made possible by window walls that go up like garage doors. At the intersection here you can take

Stocks on 2nd was one of the early entries on the street and still succeeds.

a short diversion from the Row and walk eastward, up Locust Street toward the Capitol grounds. The overflow establishments on Locust Street, next to Spice, are McGrath's Pub (another Irish bar), Carley's Ristorante, and Scott's Grille, which has been around longer than most places.

Returning to Second and continuing down toward the Hilton, you go past a convenient parking lot and the straight-forward Sandwich Man, then the in-your-face-and-mouth Dunkin' Donuts, which you will be sure to recognize by its oil-drum size coffee cup hovering overhead. Passing Commerce Bank—one of three new banks in the core of the Row—and crossing Walnut Street, you come to the Bourbon Street Saloon, which is the most recent iteration of that establishment. Next to them is Molly Brannigan's, as substantial and as Irish as Ceolta's. Both of those emerald isles, and McGrath's, are loaded with revelers during St. Patrick's Day, which seems to last a week.. Down from Brannigan's is Sam Bucca's eatery and drinkery (formerly Carmella's Trattoria), at the Market Square Plaza. Finally, you're back at the Hilton, and the relief of cool jazz outside on summer nights.

A lot of these places owe their livelihood to the new 850-space River Street parking garage that was built in the middle of the Row in 2001. It was the extra parking, the alfresco gimmick, and the lively crowd that fed the Row. "A crowd draws a crowd," said Ron Kamionka to reporter Luciew. Added Rick Galiardo, "It's the energy." Police on horseback made people feel safer (although the city unsaddled both mounts in 2008). And then there's the sex on Second. Nightlife is about sex life, or what used to be called dating, and before that, courting. If the Row were full of guys only, it might be fun at first, but eventually it would be no more stimulating than Parris Island or Devil's Island.

"Is there no end to the trendy concepts?" asked columnist Pat Carroll, on June 22, 2005.

Russ Ford, CEO of Harristown Development Corporation, another facilitator of downtown progress, said food works to draw people into the city. In short, there will be no end to the trendy concepts. "The mayor has no limit as to the number of restaurants and night spots," said Randy King, former spokesman for the Mayor, as if this extravaganza were all the doing of Stephen R. Reed.

And, in a sense, it is. Re-elected seven times since 1981, Mayor Reed has never held any job but that of elected official. During his twenty-seven year tenure as mayor, the number of businesses in the city has increased almost five-fold and property values eight-fold. Twenty-five private and public downtown projects undertaken since 1984—including the Keystone State Office Building, Pennsylvania Place apartments and offices, Forum Place, Rachel Carson state office building, Washington Square residential community, M&T Bank Tower, Harrisburg Transportation Center (the refurbished Railroad Station), Kunkel

Building, the State Employee Pension System building, Old Waterworks, Walnut Place, and the Pennsylvania Judicial Center—have totaled over 700 million dollars in value. He brought professional baseball to City Island (along with a baseball stadium); brought the National Civil War Museum to Reservoir Park; brought the Hilton Harrisburg and Crowne Plaza hotels to Market Square (he even made Market Square literally un-square); brought Whitaker Center of Science and the Arts to Market Street (he let the architect take credit for the building); and what he hopes will be his crowning achievement, Reed delivered the Harrisburg University of Science and Technology to the city's young people (whose spanking-new 16-story tower on Fourth and Market Streets downtown opened in February, 2009). The mayor was given control of the city's troubled schools by the state legislature in 2000, and he has struggled with the City Council and the School Board to keep that power and improve public education. He did place third, however, in the 2006 contest for World Mayor.

But back to Second Street. To be sure, its dining and drinking emporiums are not the only ones downtown. There are many upscale, down-scale, and off-scale opportunities that add synergy as well as provide competition for the Row. Customers can choose from institutions on Third Street (St. Moritz and Stallion's), North Street (Mangia Qui and Zephyr Express), Market Street (Gingerbread Man and Flamingo Grill), and Chestnut Street (2wentyThre3 in the Crowne Plaza hotel). The Strawberry

McGrath's on Locust Street is the third Irish pub downtown and as busy as the others.

Square complex across from the Capitol provides several shops for victuals for the Commonwealth's employees during the day, and the new Harrisburg University should generate businesses. On Walnut Street you can stop by Pep Grill, another Greek place operating since 1975, or savor the new Indian Taj Palace (formerly Sophia's Seafood) across from the Capitol. Located several blocks south of the Row in Shipoke, Char's Bella Mundo is *eccellente*, and she plans another site north of the Row at the former Tracy Mansion. But you have to start the night on Second Street, even if you finish on Third Street, or at the Police Station on Walnut Street.

In the final analysis, Second Street should not be misunderstood. These are not the sidewalk cafés of the Champs-Elysee or the Via Veneto. The festivity is not comparable to Key West or Baja. The tables slope toward the street, and so does your martini. The food smells good, but the exhaust fumes just smell. Conversation buzz is bound to compete with

Signs of the times on 2nd Street. The phrase "Restaurant Row" was first used in 1998, when the Fire House restaurant took over the site that used to be the Hope Station restaurant, and before that, Jimmy's Firehouse.

motorcycle razz. But Harrisburg hasn't seen these kinds of Second Street crowds in many, many years, going back to the holiday shopping scene downtown after World War II, which was surely a different time and place. The Row brings 6,000 to 7,000 people to the city on weekends in good weather, spending 35 to 40 million dollars annually. A city scene that some detractors used to think was *verboten* after dark could now make them say *va va voom*. Twice I have seen a bright yellow Lamborghini parked in front of Spice, protected by orange traffic cones and a maitre'd green with envy. Gracious sakes, a "Lamborghini on Second!" The last time I saw a car like that was in front of the Casino in Monte Carlo.

But if Restaurant Row is action-filled, there are places where the action has stopped. In 1977, the Catalano family opened a restaurant across the river from Harrisburg on the west shore that became a meeting place for politicians and businessmen. Catalano's was also noted for its river view and its celebrity photographs. But on New Year's Eve, 2006, Joe Catalano, descendant of the founders, said that he was closing it down because of the floods, the debt, and the competition from Restaurant Row. The Rock Bass Grill has taken its place. Diners hadn't gone to Catalano's for thirty years for the nouvelle cuisine. They went for the veal parmesan and the garlic bread, and for birthdays, anniversaries, retirement parties, and funeral luncheons. But tradition and Italian food have given way to the panache and the multicultural menu on Restaurant Row. The same fate

befell Rillo's restaurant on the west shore. The middle-aged still have their stand-bys, such as Progress Grill, Visaggio's and Tavern on the Hill some distance from downtown, but on Second Street they're not familiar with the AARP discount card.

The most famous place to shut down, even though it was located smack dab in the middle of the action, was The Spot, the legendary eatery on the northwest corner of Second and Walnut Streets. The Kaldes family or their kin had run it since 1939, first on Market Square and then at its present location, where it had to move because of construction in 1980. The Spot didn't lose to the Hilton's Golden Sheaf. It lost to the economy. "Everything is going up," Billy Kaldes told reporters Sue Gleiter and Nancy Eshelman on August 9, 2007. "There is only so much you can do with the hot dog," he said, and he had done the most with it. Their starting price in 1939 was five cents; they ended at $2.15, including the chili sauce and onions. The Spot had sold hot dogs, hamburgers and cheese steaks from the morning through the night for almost seventy years. Its regular customers ran the gamut from attorneys to hobos; the memorable patrons were the Harlem Globetrotters, the Temptations, and the Four Tops. The Spot's closing, on September 30, 2007, received top-of-the-fold, front page coverage from the *Patriot-News*. It was the kind of sentimental story a local paper likes to do.

Two years before the demise of Catalano's and the Spot, a news story on June 22, 2005, noted the other recent casualties in the restaurant trade downtown. For the historical record, here are the names, locations, and closing dates:

Gazebo Room	Second & Locust	December, 1998
Locust Street Café	Second & Locust	December, 1998
Sparky & Clark's Coffee	20 N. Second	December, 2001
Politesse	114 N. Second	December, 2001
Dewey's Dry Dock	37 N. Second	June, 2000
Zephyr Express	400 N. Second	July, 2001
Pub at 202 Locust	202 Locust	Summer, 2002
Cantone's Downtown	114 N. Second	April, 2003
The Colonnade	300 N. Second	November, 2002
The State Restaurant	409 N. Second	February, 2004
The Alley on Second	17 S. Second	Fall, 2004
Parev	215 Pine	February, 2005
Alice Anne's Kitchen	322 N. Second	March, 2005

Other restaurants that were listed in that 2005 article had closed or changed their signs by the winter of 2009—Fisaga is now Spice; Max's became Carmella's and that became Sam Bucca's; NOMA became Cabana Beach Bar, then NOMA Remixed, then Prive, and it's now Privado; 5:01 is now Bourbon Street; The Vault became Eclipse; Mezzaluna, Café Sol and Rock of Erin are changed; etcetera, etcetera. Mr. Galiardo says a normal lifecycle for a bar is about four years.

One of the notable losses is Haydn's on Pine, an upscale establishment that had taken over the building formerly occupied by Parev, which itself had been a noble effort by the grand entrepreneur John Vartan. Parev closed shortly after he died. You could spend more than a thousand dollars for a bottle of wine at Parev, but not enough people did.

The oldest surviving dining establishment downtown, on South 4th Street, next to the refurbished train station, is the Alva Restaurant. *Patriot-News* reporter Sue Gleiter tells of patrons who still come for the meatloaf, liver, crab cakes and rice pudding. Starting as a diner, it was purchased by the Giusti family in 1916; the current owners, Said and Ali Mater, bought it in 1991. Once it was open day and night, like The Spot, but that was when the trains handled loads of passengers who could be Alva customers. Today the business is slow and steady. Not trendy but dependable.

The nicest place to eat before catching the train, or after disembarking, is now Bricco's, at Third and Chestnut, only a couple of blocks from the Alva. Built in 2006 as a partnership between the Olewine School of Culinary Arts at Harrisburg Area Community College and the Hilton Harrisburg, Bricco's has succeeded. Wines sell for only ten dollars over cost, so perhaps that's what attracts the customers, besides the Mediterranean menu. Bricco's was joined by El Sol on Third Street in May, 2007.

Over ten years old now, Restaurant Row is less rowdy and more grown up. It was a good place to be on the evening of April 19, 2008. Democratic presidential candidate Barack Obama was campaigning before a throng of thousands on the Capitol steps at Third and State Streets. "Restaurant Row hopes to wine, dine, Obama's supporters," the *Patriot-News* had announced that morning, and sure enough, after his speech the crowd flowed to the Row for refreshments and fellowship. It was the kind of spring night when Spice and The Quarter rolled up their walls to be open to the street, as well as to the future. Reporter Jim Lewis interviewed a collegiate couple who had just been inspired by the Senator and who were now sipping Belgian ale in one of the new Irish pubs. Curiously but confidently, the young man opined, "I don't want to see another presidency of bipartisanship. I think Obama has the ability to bring people together." His equally curious female companion chimed in, "There's that whole cool thing now about being in politics." Likewise, we must agree, there's that whole cool thing now about being on Second Street.

XVIII

LIGHTS! CAMERA! HARRISBURG! 1896-2009

"I know, I can't believe it either," says the British Broadcasting Corporation's website on "Great Film Locations." Ranking fourth on their 2002 list of the best places to make movies is—Harrisburg, Pennsylvania! Why, on earth, Harrisburg? Because, says the BBC, Pennsylvania's capitol building is considered "one of the most beautiful in the U.S.," because "Riverside Park is also very photogenic," and because the Harrisburg State Hospital is a good place to make movies about characters who are real characters. But the clincher, they say, is because "The city is used to disruptions due to this or that protest or demonstration so the occasional movie company is handled surprisingly well."

Setting aside the question of whether or not the city should be proud of all those recommendations, let us look at the movies that have made the 'Burg something of a star. Going back to the beginnings of movie-making, we know of three short, 19th-century films that feature the city. "The Morning Alarm" (1896) is about "a December morning in Harrisburg, Pennsylvania . . . The Fire Department has received an alarm, and a crowd is gathered in the street . . . . Several large horse-drawn wagons drive past . . . ." Another ancient flick is "The First Sleigh-Ride" (1897): "In Harrisburg, Pennsylvania, normal routines are resuming after a snowstorm. . . . pedestrians watch as a vehicle passes by. But then they see something unexpected, as two sleigh drivers have decided to have a little fun on the snowy street." The plot of the third antique picture show, "Market Square, Harrisburg, Pennsylvania" (1897), filmed by the Edison Mfg. Co., is not described, but the topic sounds plain enough. They may not be Academy Award material, but these three films prove that someone was making movies here in the past. The American Film Institute notes two other historic short films featuring the city: "President McKinley's Funeral" (1901), which shows the slain president's funeral train at Harrisburg, and "Harrisburg" (1907), a 55-foot film by the S. Lubin Co. that is otherwise non-descript.

Speaking of little movies, and jumping ahead in our story, documentaries and independent films are being made in Harrisburg today. "In Heroic Fashion" was filmed in the capital city in November, 2007, by View from the Hill Productions. Put together by producer Alex Tucker, a student at the University of Connecticut, and writer-director Erick Fix, a Communications major at Messiah College in nearby Grantham, the film is about a selfish man transformed by the power of selflessness and neighborly love. More specifically, it is about a young fellow who is kidnapped and then forced to rob a bank while dressed as a superhero. The minor roles and extras

The "Girl Interrupted" film makers wanted a psychiatric hospital that sat on a hill. Scouting sites up and down the east coast, they found that the Harrisburg State Hospital worked just right. They settled in for a few months of shooting, while there were still actual patients in the hospital.

The "Girl Interrupted" stars, Winona Ryder and Angelina Jolie, stared out the hospital windows often. In the movie they were covered with sturdy screens

were filled by Harrisburg citizens, and the community also helped by donating food to the cast and crew and cutting the cost of their hotel rooms. "In Heroic Fashion" was submitted to all the major festival competitions in 2008, including Sundance. According to the Pennsylvania Film Office, other little or "indie" movies recently made in Harrisburg are "The Hungan" (also known as "Horror of the Hungry Humongous Hungan; 1991), "Superfights" (1995), "Sally" (1998), "Thomas and the Magic Railroad" (1999), "Hollywood, PA" (1999), "Through Hike—A Ghost Story" (2002), "The Vendors" (2005), "Rough Cut" (2005), and "Takedowns and Falls" (2008). Their work may never go beyond the art house or the film festival, but young filmmakers have to start somewhere, and more of them are starting in and around Harrisburg. The latest little local production is "Home," starring Oscar-winner Marcia Gay Harden, which writer/director Mary Haverstick shot in her native Lancaster County. This story of "a woman's struggle to come to terms with illness, addiction and a crumbling marriage" opened at the Midtown Cinema in Harrisburg in June, 2009. Little films tend not to be musical comedies.

The local collective ego, however, is most interested in how the major studios have used Harrisburg in major films. The earliest such example would be "Fugitive Lovers" (1934), an MGM movie starring Robert Montgomery. It's about crooks and a chorus girl on a cross-country bus trip. "Harrisburg" appears as a stop. But it wasn't really Harrisburg where they got on the bus; it was Hollywood, of course. The second big-studio picture to use Harrisburg somehow was "Ceiling Zero" (1936), produced by Warner Brothers, directed by Howard Hawks, and starring Jimmy Cagney and Pat O'Brien. This is a movie about brave pilots, hazardous flying conditions, and a de-icing gadget. "Harrisburg" figures as an airport, or perhaps they just fly over it. But again, nothing really happens there because Harrisburg isn't really in the movie. It's just a hook for some of the events in the plot.

A light comedy that pretends to take place in Harrisburg is "The Remarkable Mr. Pennypacker" (1959) starring the imperious Clifton Webb. This is the story of a businessman in the 1890s who commutes between two different offices, in two different cities, because he has two different families unbeknownst to one another. But then they become beknownst to one another, and the fun begins. The home base for his bigamy is Harrisburg, while he keeps the other family in Philadelphia. Horace Pennypacker is a free-thinking supporter of women's suffrage and Darwinism, so you might think he would be more at home in Philadelphia than Harrisburg, but locating the story in Harrisburg gives the movie the backdrop of middle-class propriety it needs. Ultimately, the Philadelphia branch of the family moves to Harrisburg, and Pennypacker's 17 children live here happily ever after. Regardless, the Catholic church disapproved of "Pennypacker."

A special case in local film history is a movie modeled on Harrisburg although the place is not called Harrisburg. We are talking about "A Rage to Live" (1965), a steamy melodrama based on John O'Hara's best-selling novel of the same name, written in 1949. O'Hara did not try to conceal Harrisburg completely in the book. Indeed, in his novel's introductory "Note," he writes, "Harrisburg is one of my favorite cities . . . But because this is a work of fiction I had had to

obliterate Harrisburg and Dauphin and the Susquehanna and substitute Fort Penn and Nesquehela, county and river. I also have made a complete substitution of the population past and present of Harrisburg and Dauphin County, and anyone who thinks he sees himself or anyone else in this novel is wrong."

Of course, that's what any writer would say before he makes ugly characters out of real people. Prof. Irwin Richman of Penn State Harrisburg recalls a conversation he had with Pennsylvania historian Donald Kent in the 1960s, who told him that guessing the true identities of "Rage to Live" characters had been a popular parlor game in the city for some time. The citizens of Harrisburg didn't trust O'Hara's denials anymore than did the folks in Pottsville. That's the town O'Hara came from, a place that scorned him because they thought he had written about them scornfully.

In any case, Harrisburg's image is vital to the "Rage" plot because the drama needs a platform for upper-class decadence. Fort Penn is the hometown of Grace Caldwell Tate, a rich nymphomaniac, played by Suzanne Pleshette. "She needed love like some women needed whiskey," says the admonishing voiceover in the movie's trailer. *Variety* cleverly called it "a banal transfer from tome to film," but the movie's failure did not mean O'Hara had failed as a novelist in describing Fort Penn/Harrisburg. *The New*

The grounds surrounding the Harrisburg State Hospital are verdant and rather forbidding.

There was no "Administration" sign on the main building at the hospital, so the "Girl Interrupted" Art Department made one and put it up. John Pufnak, current Safety Inspector at the facility, says that about ten major and minor films have been made there, including "Girl Interrupted" and, most recently, "Another Harvest Moon," where the hospital plays a nursing home.

Yorker reviewer wrote that "The range of O'Hara's knowledge of how Americans live was incomparably greater than that of any other fiction writer of his time," and *The New York Times Book Review* judged that "Like Dreiser and Sinclair Lewis before him, [O'Hara] was determined to record the whole of American life." So let it be said that John O'Hara, literary anthropologist, got to Harrisburg one way or another at mid-century.

Another special case is a movie that never mentions Harrisburg, and that never happened in Harrisburg, but makes people think of Harrisburg. In the spring of 1979, the Academy Award-winning "China Syndrome," starring Jack Lemmon and Jane Fonda, opened on theater screens only twelve days before the nuclear accident at Three Mile Island, only a few miles from Harrisburg. The coincidence turned out to be unnerving. Harrisburg has been forever associated with "Syndrome" not only because of the film's timing with the accident but also because Harrisburg was the largest city near

the nuclear plant, and because one of the lines in the movie mentions an impending devastation that will be "the size of Pennsylvania." At least the accident hasn't been named after Harrisburg. Incidentally, the image of TMI shows up most recently in "X-Men Origins: Wolverine" (2009), when Wolverine fights Sabretooth and Deadpool in a climactic battle on top of one of the cooling towers. Superhero Hugh Jackman, however, never actually came to Middletown for the scene. It was all fake.

Harrisburg's career as a genuine film location began in the 1990s (not counting the charming teen romance "Mannequin," partly filmed inside Boscov's department store in Camp Hill in 1987). "The Distinguished Gentleman" (1992) is an Eddie Murphy vehicle about a conman who gets elected to Congress. The film used the city and the capitol complex extensively for sets and backdrops suggesting Washington. Critics treated it as

another Murphy flop, but the Political Film Society gave it a special award.

"Major League II" (1994), a sequel to a zany baseball comedy, was the next film to be located in the city. Starring Charlie Sheen, Tom Berenger and Corbin Bernsen, the same trio that made the first version successful, #II was shot on Harrisburg's City Island baseball field. Only native Harrisburgers would recognize that the palm trees had been imported to create a convincing spring-training ambience.

"Girl Interrupted" (1999) qualifies as the most significant film to use Harrisburg as a production site. Here the Harrisburg State Hospital is not only convenient scenery but an institution crucial to the plot. Based on Susanna Kaysen's reminiscence, the film tells of the time she spent in a psychiatric hospital in the 1960s for treatment of Borderline Personality Disorder. The city was celebrity-filled for this one: Winona Ryder plays the part of Kaysen, Vanessa Redgrave is her psychiatrist, Whoopi Goldberg is the helpful nurse in the ward, and Angelina Jolie is the resident sociopath. Both Redgrave and Goldberg had won Oscars previously, and Jolie was so convincing in her role that she received the Academy Award as Best Actress in a Supporting Role.

This film looks right too—the place is rather bucolic but still rather confining. The art director re-landscaped some of the grounds, so HSH is not a scary "Snake Pit," the name of the 1948 film, starring Olivia de Havilland, which exposed wretched mental hospitals. However, neither is HSH the mirror image of Bette Davis's posh sanitarium in "Now, Voyager" (1942), for the windows in the "Girl Interrupted" wards have very thick screens on them. Off the grounds, the Bellevue Park home of Prof. Winston and Kathleen Richards was used for a psychiatrist's office in the film. Winston recalls how thoroughly *apropos* his house and their Harrisburg neighborhood looked when the set designers were done with their work. All the cars and clothes were the right vintage, and even the bookshelves in the psychiatrist's office (Winston's own home office) were re-stocked with volumes published no later than the Sixties. Locals will recognize the proximate spot where Ms. Ryder sits overlooking a Susquehanna River bridge, and they should also identify Main Street in Mechanicsburg. Unfortunately, Ms. Ryder dissed Harrisburg afterwards because it failed to entertain her on the weekends.

The Harrisburg State Hospital was used again as a film location in June, 2008, for "Another Harvest Moon." This time the place played the part of a nursing home, so the stars were older too—Ernest Borgnine, Anne Meara, Doris Roberts, and Cybil Shepherd. The director, Camp Hill native Greg Swartz, commented "This area is underrepresented in film. There are stories to be told here." Not all of them through the State Hospital, one hopes.

Harrisburg should truly regret that it showed up in "8MM" (1999). Nicholas Cage, a surveillance specialist "living in the suburbs of Harrisburg, Pennsylvania," is hired to investigate the murder of a girl who was deliberately killed

Scenes for "Another Harvest Moon" were filmed in this room at the former Harrisburg State Hospital. HSH no longer houses psychiatric patients and is now used by the state's Department of General Services.

to make a film, which leads him into the smarmicst corners of contemporary culture. Some Harrisburg landmarks appear in "8MM," as well as a *Patriot-News* front page. While Cage is uncomfortably watching the guilty "snuff film" for clues, he is seen wearing a Penn State sweatshirt. Perhaps somebody from Pitt provided that prop.

"Lucky Numbers" (1999) was another picture located in Harrisburg that qualifies as a special case because it was based on an event that actually happened—the effort to fix a Pennsylvania State Lotto jackpot drawing and the resultant scandal in 1988. It features superstars John Travolta, Lisa Kudrow, Tim Roth, and Bill Pullman, all directed by Nora Ephron. Travolta plays the part of a popular TV weatherman who has a sideline business in snowmobiles that's failing. He first tries to recoup his losses by burglarizing the business for the insurance proceeds, and when that fails, he talks his girlfriend into helping rig the lottery, a scheme that eventually comes apart too, as does the film. Harrisburg *Patriot-News* film critic

Sharon Johnson was not amused by this dark screwball comedy. This was another instance, she wrote, in which "the city and its residents are abused." *New York Times* critic Elvis Mitchell backed her up, saying Ms. Ephron, with this "novel adventure in slumming," had made Harrisburg a "tacky trash outpost" where "loser culture" held sway.

Such treatment of the capital city brings up for discussion several films where the mere mention of the word "Harrisburg" is intended to convey an image. This is not counting "East Side Kids" (1940), whose cast lists an actor named "Harris Berger," nor are we including the 1984 German film, "Die Letzte Fahrt nach Harrisburg" (The Last Trip to Harrisburg). Neither does this discussion include the films "The Fabulous Dorseys" (1947) and "The Light in the Forest" (1958), which had their world premieres in Harrisburg but no filming there.

The first example of Just-Say-Harrisburg movies is Alfred Hitchcock's trademark thriller, "The Man Who Knew Too Much" (1956). It stars the all-American performers James Stewart and Doris Day, who play an all-American couple in trouble overseas. Stewart's character is Dr. Ben McKenna, a straight-forward general surgeon, and Miss Day plays the part of Jo, his spouse and a former songstress. After attending a medical convention in Paris, Ben, Jo and their son Hank take a vacation in Marrakech, Morocco, where they happen to witness a murder. Their son is then kidnapped to keep the parents quiet about what they know. Trying to track down their son, the parents follow the trail to London, where they happen to run into some American friends. Ben makes small talk with them in his hotel room. He is introduced to "Cindy Fontaine, from Harrisburg, PA."

"Oh, Harrisburg?" says Stewart, as if he knew the city well (he could have—Stewart was a native of Indiana, Pennsylvania). "Been back home lately?" he asks.

"How can I?" says Cindy. "They know me there as Elva McDuff. It doesn't quite fit me any more."

All that's missing from the soundtrack is the drummer's rim shot—ding! The woman was home-spun Elva McDuff when she lived in plain old Harrisburg, but now she's acquired some European *savoir-faire*, so she's the *trés chic* Cindy Fontaine. Hitchcock lets us know with one quick line that the prodigal daughter had better not return to the 'Burg if she wants to keep her stylish new status.

The Just-Say-Harrisburg motif is evident again in the strangely titled "Sheila Levine is Dead and Living in New York" (1975), where Jeannie Berlin plays the part of a bright but painfully shy girl who moves from Harrisburg to the Big Apple. She meets and falls for Dr. Sam Stoneman, played by the late Roy Scheider, whose usual greeting to her is, "How are you, Harrisburg?" Sheila eventually gains confidence and values herself, but her role and her nickname are not exactly a compliment to the city.

The next example of negative name-dropping is found in "Animal House," the big-hit college fraternity movie of 1978, which was rated #1 on Bravo's "100 Funniest Movies" list. (The film was rated only the 36th funniest movie by the serious-minded American Film Institute, but what would they know?). As the Delta brothers are viewing slides of freshmen they might pick for membership, one chubby nerd's picture comes up, and the Rush Chairman identifies him as "Kent Dorfman—he's a legacy from Harrisburg," whereupon all the brothers shout protests and throw beer cans at the screen. But they pledge him anyway, and the freshman happily plods through the rest of the movie. But we might ask the film's director, John Landis, couldn't you have had Kent come from Cleveland?

Tim Robbins' political satire, "Bob Roberts," (1992) is a "mockumentary" developed from a sketch Robbins had done for "Saturday Night Live." He refers to Harrisburg in the script because the film's campaign action takes place in Pennsylvania. Fortunately, his humorous barbs were never thrown directly at the 'Burg.

The Just-Say-Harrisburg list goes on. In "Ed" (2000), Tom Cavanaugh plays the character of Ed Stevens, who has returned to Stuckeyville, his hometown, to open up a law practice in a bowling alley. Quirky Ed says to his old girlfriend, "That's right, you could move away to Guam, Borneo, Harrisburg, Pennsylvania, God knows where. The truth is you'll be making a beeline right back to Stuckeyville." Is he implying that Harrisburg is as exotic as Borneo, or that it's precisely un-exotic? In either case, the reference is not meant to be appealing to the audience.

In the slice-of-American-life movie "Diamond Men" (2000), Bobby Walker, played by Donnie

Angelina Jolie and a male suitor used this fire escape in "Girl Interrupted."

the witchcraft of the combination? Does the suffix "burg," like "ville," now routinely connote bumpkinry? In the original German, the term "burg" can refer to "castle" or "fortress," which would seem to be the opposite of yokeldom. Ach du Lieber! (Oh, Heavens!) What have we done to deserve this?

Even at the cutting edge of comedy the affront can be found. The city was mentioned in 1997 in the 179th episode of "The Simpsons" as a weird detail in a flashback: Says Homer, "(Sigh) It's about time I told you about a chapter of my life that I had hoped would be closed forever. I was on my way to the Harrisburg coat outlet to buy an irregular coat." To be in Harrisburg is to be on sale and irregular, in other words. At the same time, in autumn, 1997, making one think it was part of a coordinated conspiracy, the city was cited in a phony news flash on "The Onion," the famous comic website: "In a deal that has sent shock waves through the entertainment industry, Cineplex Odeon, the nation's second-largest movie-theater chain, has agreed in principle to a 10-picture, $70 deal with Harrisburg, PA, bank teller Douglas Phelps."

One might say it is prestige of a sort for Harrisburg to be considered a comic device by the writers of blockbuster movies, "indie" films, witty TV shows, and ersatz newspapers. However, the moral of these messages might be that Harrisburg should re-name itself if it wants to continue re-making itself. But I say we don't need a new moniker concocted by some real estate developer who might try to conjure up the image of a quaint English village by calling

Wahlberg, gives mock praise to the city when he says, "I tell ya, the girls in these *%#+holes, they got nothing better to do. It's not like they're living in Harrisburg or something." Wouldn't "living in Albany" have worked just as well?

How did Harrisburg's name turn into a punch line? Is this the new Newark? Are the screenwriters enticed by the sounds/ Harris/ and /burg/, or is it just the capital "Sherwood Glen" or whatever. Instead, we can re-brand the city quite authentically by restoring its original name. I suggest that Harrisburg hereafter be called "Harris Ferry," as it was known in the graceful eighteenth century.

Think it over. The pairing of those two-syllable words is rhythmically balanced—Har-ris Fer-ry, one-two, one-two. The four /r/s trip off the tongue easily—rah-rah, rah-rah. Misspellings hereafter will be rare—how often now is our name written Harrisburgh, as if it were Pittsburgh? The subjective associations of this old-cum-new name would all be positive—imagine the Harris Ferry as a gaily-painted little vessel floating down the river's sparkling waters, the passengers chuckling when her whistle toots, and everyone on board feeling cheery for the whole cruise. Which is exactly right now the impact our own riverboat, the Pride of the Susquehanna. Rename it "Harris Ferry" too, to match the city and provide us with a logo. Finally, to be practical, look how economic conditions improved when Delaware Township, New Jersey, took the new title "Cherry Hill," and when North Tarrytown, New York, decided to call itself "Sleepy Hollow." Jernigan, Florida they reconstituted as "Orlando," to its profound advantage. And remember the excitement when Hot Springs, New Mexico, changed its name to "Truth or Consequences"? Well, maybe re-naming doesn't always work, but it might be worth a try.

Restaurant Row on North Second Street has yet to appear in a movie, but that may be only a matter of time.

"Shocker!" exclaimed *The Patriot-News* on Wednesday, May 20, 2009. In the previous day's primary election, City Council President Linda D. Thompson had upset Harrisburg's "Mayor for Life" Stephen R. Reed. The results couldn't be called close: Thompson thumped Reed 3,496 votes to 2,438, or 55% to 38% of the Democratic electorate. Thompson won 19 precincts or wards and Reed only 9. He prevailed among whites in the midtown, Bellevue Park and northernmost areas of the city, as well as in Shipoke along the southern riverside (he won 87 to 13 in that neighborhood); her campaign turned out black voters in the rest of the city, particularly in the more populous uptown and Allison Hill sections. Thompson's primary victory, however, was not just a consummation of racial politics, nor was it simply the first successful effort by an African American woman in a mayoralty race. Her triumph finally relied upon

Mayor Reed's obstacles and gaffes, either real or imagined. The City Council President had aimed her criticism at the Mayor's proposed Wild West museum that never worked, and then at the costly city incinerator that seemed unworkable. If she frequently lacked eloquence, she was nevertheless effectively caustic. And the Mayor, it appears, hadn't worked hard enough on his campaign himself. Pre-election polls had him leading Thompson 44 percent to 29 percent and raising twice as much campaign money as she had. So what was there to worry about? He had never lost an election in his political life, and he nearly always won both the Democratic and Republican Party's nominations in the mayoral primary. But Thompson's campaigners, said the *Patriot-News,* pursued a strategy that left Reed's team "flatfooted by comparison." Her workers "were seen approaching groups of youths on the streets, asking them if they were registered." Her top campaign adviser, James Ellison, said, "Those kids went all over the city. They went to the south side, they walked up to every apartment in Hall Manor [the public housing complex], and they banged on every door." Said Diane Bowman, chairwoman of the Democratic Party in Dauphin County, "I think this election definitely showed a message of change, a carryover from the Obama campaign. People had more than they wanted of incumbencies." In other words, one could say Reed lost because he had won so often. Among the changes Thompson promised were a new Harrisburg School District Superintendent and a new Chief of Police. Chief

Charles G. Kellar immediately announced his plans to retire.

The farewells and festschrifts to the Mayor came quickly. "City turns from mayor who made it," headlined the *Sunday Patriot-News* on May 24th. "Reed put city back on its feet," was the title of former editor Dale Davenport's commentary inside the paper. Letters to the editor and messages on Pennlive.com praised his undeniable accomplishments, from re-starting City Island and the Harrisburg Senators baseball team to cementing the Hilton Harrisburg and the downtown's new look. At the same time, one could read or hear discouraging and discourteous words about the future. "Give Thompson a chance," said one commentator, which was strange praise in light of her landslide victory.

In early June, Mayor Reed said he might think about running a write-in campaign for the general election on November 3, 2009. His campaign manager, Randy King, said they had been "inundated" with pleas that Reed throw his hat back into the ring. Running as the Republican nominee was unlikely, as Reed had also lost that party's primary to Nevin Mindlin, 422 to 335, and Mindlin said he was staying in the race. At one point, Reed was quoted as saying "I have not given more than one hour's thought to the whole thing."

Whatever happens, as one politician said after the primary results were in, "Oh, my!" Yes, we can all agree with that instant analysis and tentative forecast for the capital city: Oh, my!

The smartly dressed staff of a tailor shop pose in front of their store at S. Third Street and Blackberry Alley in this 1900 photo. Small-scale entrepreneurs have always contributed a great deal to Harrisburg, including a strong foundation for the area's commercial community. (HSDC)

XIX

CHRONICLES OF LEADERSHIP

Harrisburg was destined by geography to be a distribution center, and the highway network that so efficiently ties these diverse communities together is itself part of the regional heritage. Natural roads travel north-south, skirting the eastern edge of the Appalachian mountain range. And the best east-west route through the mountains also crosses Harrisburg.

During the great canal era of American commerce, greater Harrisburg was a hub and trans-shipment center. The Pennsylvania Canal crossed the Susquehanna at Clarks Ferry; the Penn Lock was located near Walnut Street in the capitol complex. And the Union Canal joined the Susquehanna at Middletown, connecting to the Schuylkill River at Reading.

Harrisburg's highway network now includes the Pennsylvania Turnpike and several other major interstate highways. They continued the tradition (and usually follow the same routes) of the Indian paths, pioneer roads, and canals that preceded them. Amtrak and Conrail transport passengers and freight along rights-of-way once followed by trains of Conestoga wagons.

German immigrants pushing west from the crowded lands of the Atlantic Coast area knew that by following the black walnut trees, they would find the richest, most fertile soils. That custom led them to Lancaster County, then up the Susquehanna Valley to Harrisburg and into the West. That rich soil and agricultural heritage have made central Pennsylvania a leading food producer. Agriculture, food processing, and food distribution are still the way many area residents earn their daily bread.

Greater Harrisburg is a complex society. State government dominates the region, but private industry remains powerful and active. The people of central Pennsylvania are proud and hard working. There is a tradition of self-reliance, productivity, and craftsmanship that goes back 150 years or more.

Change comes slowly in central Pennsylvania, for there is respect for the old—the known, tried, and proven. Only when newcomers— new people, new industries, new ideas—prove themselves are they accepted fully as community partners. Yet there is also a real belief in progress and a desire to be up to date and in tune with the times.

Local social customs require gracious understatement and modesty. Harrisburg's business and professional leaders are reluctant to parade their achievements. But there is also respect for family and associates, and a deep appreciation of history.

The pages that follow are a tribute to past generations of vision, work, and dedication. They are offered so that future generations may understand and share greater Harrisburg's traditions, heritage, and community pride.

ANGINO & ROVNER

By the time Richard Angino was 13, he was setting pins in a Duquesne bowling alley from 6:30 p.m. until closing time, as well as all day on weekends, jumping lanes and earning 8 cents a line (game), $5 a night and $15 a weekend. Today, as an attorney he knows that modern child labor laws would never allow a youngster of 13 to exhibit the scrappy work ethic he developed at so young an age. As senior attorney and owner of Angino & Rovner, a successful civil litigation firm in Harrisburg, Pennsylvania, and as a horticulturalist and philanthropist, he looks back at an unconventional life that offered him so many character-building opportunities.

Growing up poor in Duquesne, outside of Pittsburgh, Richard lost his father when he was three and was raised by his mother and siblings. In 1952 at the end of the Korean War, an older brother in the American Red Cross brought the family to Japan for a year. Richard, who was 12 then, was educated in a one-room school house. Back in the States, his freshman and sophomore years were spent studying for the priesthood at St. Gregory's Seminary in Cincinnati, Ohio.

In his junior year and for four consecutive years, Richard spent his summers working 14 hour days, seven days a week, as the "Voice" of Kenneywood, an amusement park in Pittsburgh. "I made all the public service announcements for the park," Angino recalls with fondness, "lost children, special events, playing music, closing time. It was a prestigious position because everyone heard my voice."

A good athlete who did well in school, Richard nonetheless had little knowledge of the world of professional careers. He went to college with the vague idea of becoming a teacher when a fortuitous conversation changed his life. "I was approached my senior year by someone who talked to me about the law as a continuation of my education that could lead to many opportunities," he recalls. "You could go into the political arena,

Richard Angino and his wife, Alice.

the public sector or into private practice." Richard began to see how a law degree could be the foundation for a multitude of careers, including running businesses and corporations. "It made sense to me and, since I wasn't ready to make a career commitment at that time, I decided to go to law school."

Richard graduated seventh in his class Law Review from Villanova Law School in Philadelphia in 1965 and immediately went to work for Hurwitz, Klein, Meyers and Benjamin in Harrisburg where his career kicked into gear quickly. A general practice law firm, the founder, Solomon Hurwitz, died shortly after Richard came on board leaving a void on the business side that none of the other lawyers seemed willing or able to fill. "I was young enough to be able to take on the decision-making abilities and to bring in the money," says Angino. "Within three years I was running the place."

"Running the place" meant eventually narrowing the firm's focus from a broad range of general practice activities to a highly focused civil litigation practice. "Because I was doing most of the work I

quickly concentrated on civil litigation and focused the firm that way."

In doing so, Richard was responding in some way to his background. Growing up poor in a steel town he had always felt a sense of exclusion. Civil litigation allowed him to act on behalf of people who didn't have the means of defending themselves against the big guy. "We litigate on behalf of innocent victims," he says, "People who are injured because of the negligence of others. The defendant could be a doctor or General Motors; the plaintiff an elderly person who takes her CDs to a financial advisor who puts her money into a risky investment and loses it. The people we represent are the victims of someone else's actions."

When Pennsylvania passed a no-fault auto insurance law in 1974, Richard argued that the families of deceased victims should be able to collect for their lost earnings the same as living injured victims. "I took that interpretation all the way to the Pennsylvania Supreme Court and obtained a favorable decision." He was then able to bring class action suits against insurance companies and recover millions on behalf of thousands of victims. During his 1982 term as president of the Pennsylvania Trial Lawyers Richard negotiated the 1984 Automobile

View of the Pergolas and Pavilions of the Italian Garden at Felicita.

Law. The firm grew quickly and Angino & Rovner became a recognized name throughout Pennsylvania and eventually four of the firm's eight attorneys were recognized among the 53 best plaintiffs' lawyers in Pennsylvania.

Richard's wife, Alice, who came to work for him as a secretary in 1968, is Richard's partner not only in running the firm where Alice serves as legal administrator, but also in their shared passions for gardening and philanthropy that have grown into major endeavors.

In 1971 the couple bought a 52-acre abandoned farm and began the process of transforming it into extensive gardens. "If you can picture an attorney and his wife being happy putting all their money into gardening and philanthropy, that's what we've done," says Richard, who moved through the chairs of the American Horticultural Society, rising to the position of vice president. Together, Richard and Alice traveled throughout France, Italy, England, Holland, and Germany, studying the grand European gardens for inspiration. "We've tried over the years to create something that approaches these great gardens."

Today, the gardens have expanded to include Felicita Resort, a spa and golf get-away in Central Pennsylvania.

From the '70s to the present, the Anginos have contributed to and/or landscaped many Central Pennsylvania capital charitable projects in county parks (Fort Hunter, Wildwood, Wiconisco) and non-profits (Cerebral Palsy, YWCA, Colonial Park Library, Gaudenzia, United Way, Good Shepherd School, Association of Retarded Citizens Camp Sertoma, etc.)

The Anginos also combined their gardens and philanthropy by hosting and underwriting themed fundraisers held in the gardens for numerous charities including The Frederick Michael Angino Pediatric Leukemia Fund at Hershey Medical Center, The Greater Harrisburg Foundation, Open Stage of Harrisburg, United Way, Pennsylvania Breast Cancer Coalition, etc.

Richard and Alice have been long time strong supporters, both financially and through board service, of many non-profits in their community, including Tocqueville Society of the United Way, Allied Arts, Harrisburg Symphony Society, National Multiple Sclerosis Society, Leukemia and Lymphoma Society, Wildwood Lake Nature Center, Boys and Girls Club, St. Francis of Assisi Children's Summer Program, etc.

Looking forward through green-tinted glasses, the Anginos are now creating a 21st Century, green, sustainable carbon-neutral development of cottages and villas with a retail component of shops and theaters where present and future generations can enjoy the good life. Their l987 Will provides for the gardens to be perpetually maintained as a trust ensuring that the Angino's impact on Harrisburg will continue for many years to come.

HARRISBURG AREA COMMUNITY COLLEGE (HACC)

Harrisburg Area Community College (HACC) became Pennsylvania's first community college when it was chartered in February 1964 to serve the residents of Cumberland, Dauphin and Perry counties.

HACC was established under the leadership of college founders Bruce E. Cooper and James W. Evans who shared a dream of creating an "opportunity school" for students of all ages from all walks of life. The college had tremendous support from the community, and the financial backing of local school districts and the state.

HACC opened its doors to the first class of 465 students in 1964 in two buildings at the former Harrisburg Academy on North Front Street (now the site of Dixon University Center). In 1965 when Hershey Junior College closed, most of the school's faculty and students joined HACC. With the Hershey students and a larger than anticipated freshman class, enrollment soared to 1,314 in fall 1965 and the college added two more buildings. Planning was already under way for a permanent campus on 157 acres

HACC's Rose Lehrman Arts Center, right, was added in 1975, and the Helen Y. Swope Carillon/Clocktower was dedicated in 1987.

A new Chain of Office was presented to HACC President Edna V. Baehre, Ph.D., left, on the occasion of her 10th anniversary at the helm of Central Pennsylvania's Community College. Accompanying Dr. Baehre are Board of Trustees Chairman Donald Schell, center, and the late Trustee Chairman Emeritus James Evans, Ph.D.

in Wildwood Park sold to HACC by the City of Harrisburg for $1 in March 1965. Thirteen months later, ground was broken for a $3.5 million building project. The first classes on the new campus opened in 1967.

In anticipation of the expanding role of technology in the workplace, HACC broke ground for the state's first community college technology center in 1984. The Hall Technology Center, named for benefactor John N. Hall, was the college hub for high-tech programs, computer-assisted drafting and electronics for more than two decades. In 2001, HACC opened a Midtown site that now includes the original AMP, Inc. headquarters and the newest addition, the former Evangelical Press Building that opened in 2007. The two buildings house HACC's trades and technologies programs as well as evolving programs in "green" technology.

The HACC Foundation was established in 1985 as a non-profit educational trust. In 1992, the foundation was ranked as the largest community college endowment in the nation by the Council for Aid to Education. Today, more than 200 endowments support a diverse range of college needs including scholarships, capital equipment, international education and academic programs.

In 1988, HACC again responded to community need for education and training when it opened its Public Safety Center (PSC). Located on 12 acres of the Harrisburg Campus, the center provides entry-level and advanced training for professionals in fire/rescue, law enforcement, emergency medical services/healthcare and automotive training. Each year, the center offers nearly 2,000 training programs to 38,000 students from a 14-county region. The majority of Central Pennsylvania's municipal police officers, emergency responders and firefighters are trained and graduate from the PSC, earning state and national certification as well as credits toward an associate degree. HACC's Police Academy is the second largest in the state. HACC also operates a nationally recognized polygraph school that serves the northeastern United States. In 2000, the center was renamed the Senator John J. Shumaker Public Safety Center in honor of the Harrisburg legislator instrumental in its establishment.

In the two decades since, HACC's growth has expanded to include five regional campuses, and the college has become known as HACC, Central Pennsylvania's Community College. Gettysburg and Lancaster opened in 1989, followed by Lebanon a year later. Three months after the Lebanon Campus opened, it was destroyed by fire. Efforts to rebuild began almost immediately and a new campus on the original site opened in January 1992. That same year, the Harrisburg Campus opened Mumma Hall/C. Ted Lick Wildwood Conference Center, followed by the Benjamin Olewine III School of Culinary Arts. In 1997, Gettysburg moved to its current campus location on Old Harrisburg Road and subsequently has undergone major expansions and renovations. In 2001, the Lancaster Campus moved to its current location on Old Philadelphia Pike, expanding three years later. In 2003, the York Center was established, moving in August 2005 to Pennsylvania Avenue and becoming a campus in 2007.

A student in HACC's dental assistant associate degree program works on a patient in the college's Dental Clinic in the Select Medical Health Education Pavilion.

A group of HACC students gather on the lawn in front of Cooper Student Center.

When Clyde E. Blocker agreed to be HACC's first president in May 1964, he proclaimed, "I believe that the community college in the Harrisburg region can stimulate a resurgence of education and cultural activity which will touch upon the lives of all citizens in the area."

The foundation upon which HACC was built continues today under the leadership of Edna V. Baehre, Ph.D., who has been HACC's president since 1997. "Community colleges have been called the Ellis Island of higher education, the place where those who come from many shores and many corners of society have a chance at living the American dream through education," she said. Community colleges provide "an education that increases literacy and the ability to communicate, an education that teaches skills in order to enter jobs with family sustaining wages, and an education that shapes the minds of students to increase awareness about the world, its human conditions and philosophies of the past and present."

In seeking to fulfill its mission of "providing education and cultural opportunities to the community it serves," HACC has become one of the largest undergraduate colleges in Pennsylvania as well as being the largest provider of non-credit workforce training in the state. The college offers nearly 200 associate degree, certificate and diploma programs to more than 21,000 credit students and 50,000 noncredit and workforce development students on its five regional campuses and in community locations in an eight-county area. A Virtual Campus established in 2005 offers a wide range of online courses globally.

HACC continues to enjoy a broad base of community support. Through the strong leadership of the board of trustees, the outstanding support of The HACC Foundation, and vital partnerships with school districts, businesses and the higher education community, HACC has established itself as a leader in providing high-quality, affordable education, training the workforce and improving the quality of life in the region.

HACC's nearly 40,000 alumni have achieved distinction in almost every field, including business, medicine, law, the arts, education, public service, the military and the technologies.

For more information, go to www.hacc.edu.

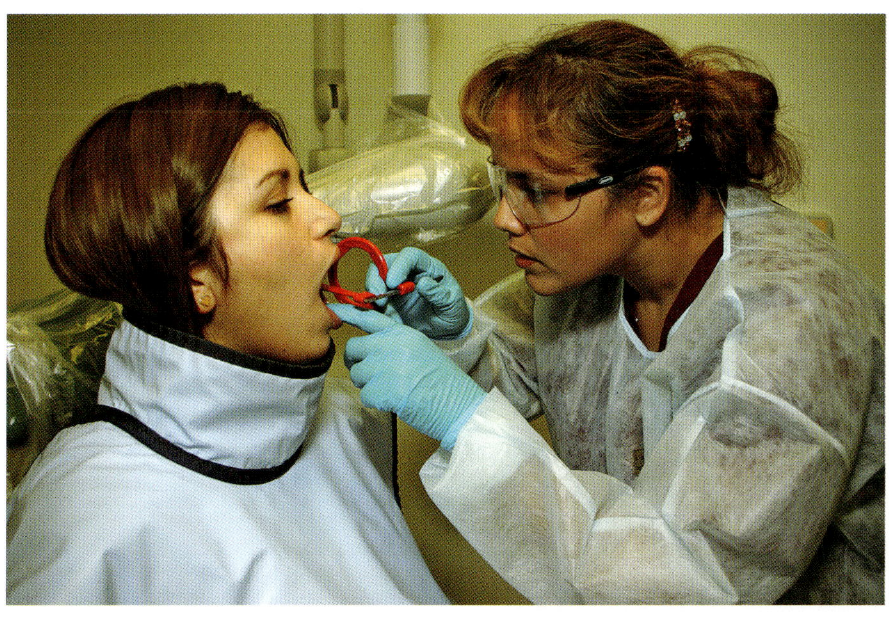

LIGHTSTYLES, LTD

Helping to shed light on the walls of history, LightStyles LTD distributes custom-made windows and doors, including historic replications of expertly crafted, high-end windows and doors to retailers up and down the east coast. LightStyles, located at 1261 Claremont Road in Carlisle, Pennsylvania is a distribution company specializing in providing made-to-order windows and doors, as well as modern style new and replacement windows and doors for homes, commercial structures, major universities and government buildings. LightStyles is one of the top five distribution houses for the distinguished Marvin Windows and Doors product line that provides not only quality products, but a sense of heritage for its customers.

Robert L. Slagle grasped the need for such a distribution house that could specialize and accommodate the requirements of this high-end market. Slagle was never a stranger to hard work. Born in Abbottsville, Pennsylvania, young Robert (Bob) and his family soon moved to Dillsburg where they owned and operated a dairy farm. He helped work the farm at the young age of 9; milking cows, operating equipment, and contributing in every way he could to all phases of the family business. He worked on the farm until he completed his schooling at Northern High School.

Soon after graduation, Bob went to work for a contractor. He learned quickly

Smyser Iron Works restored by Kinsley Construction featuring historically replicated windows by Marvin Windows and Doors.

and became skilled as both a framer and finish carpenter. By 18, he was adept at all aspects of building houses.

Bob was always interested in learning all facets of a business. When he was working with his family, he studied farming. When building houses, he was mindful of materials, suppliers and labor. It was through this natural curiosity that he began to look for ways to advance his career and create his own place in business.

Through his work for the contractor, Bob established a relationship with a building supply company called The Lumber Yard where he went to work at age 20. He was employed there for almost two years. Soon after, Bob landed a job at Morgan Millwork Company, eventually called Morgan Distribution, where his first duty was as a billing clerk. He advanced through the ranks of the company for almost 25 years, learning the processes of supply and distribution. Bob clearly learned well and he eventually became president of the company.

Bob saw a growth opportunity at another company called Adam Wholesaler. He began working for the company and quickly advanced to eastern regional vice president. The company worked with established lines like Andersen Windows and other building supply lines. After working for the company for nine years, Bob felt that there was a need for a high-end window line that Andersen had not yet managed to produce. He encouraged the company to add the prestigious Marvin Windows and Doors line to meet the demand for specialty products in the historical refurbishing market. The Adam's Company, influenced by Bob's urging, bought the Lynchburg, Virginia franchise in August 1992. A few short years after, it was decided that the Marvin Windows and Doors line was a conflict of interest for the company's other lines. The Marvin Windows and Doors line was dropped from Adam Wholesaler.

Bob Slagle then made a decision that would change the course of his life and career forever. In 1995, he left Adam Wholesaler and created his own company, LightStyles, LTD. His new company catered specifically to high-end retailers whose customers were in need of historical reproductions of windows and doors and other modern, custom-made designs for hardware, windows and doors.

The 1790s Farm House restored by Kinsley Construction featuring historically replicated windows by Marvin Windows and Doors.

In this endeavor, Bob had a partner, his wife Susan, vice president of the company. Susan encouraged him every step of the way. It was her enthusiasm and insight that helped form the philosophy for the company and creatively conceived a perfect name for the new business. The name had to express that windows and doors truly create a mood and tell a story of how light shines through into a home or building. She thought about it and came up with LightStyles, a name that captures the idea of how many styles of light are created when the sun shines into a home.

The market for high-end, custom-made windows clearly was present and regional retailers knew where to find them – LightStyles, LTD. Supplying historical reproductions of windows and doors quickly became the company's specialty. LightStyles has been instrumental in recreating windows and doors that were more than 250 years old. Some of their most respected projects include recreating windows and doors in old farmhouses dating back to the 1700's, historic government buildings and homes registered in the National Historic Registrar. One such building is the beautifully refurbished Smyser Building in York, Pennsylvania. Another example is the historic York County Library on Market Street.

LightStyles has been distinguished by the *Central Pennsylvania Journal* as one of the region's Fastest Growing Companies, two years in a row. The company's territory covers South Central Pennsylvania, Maryland, West Virginia, District of Columbia, Virginia, North Carolina and South Carolina. More than 100 employees are part of the "LightStyles Family," which is how Bob Slagle refers to his valued team.

As founder of the company, Bob has a strong foundation born from his expertise, dedication and commitment to his retailers. He is mindful of the changing needs of customers and confidently plans to accommodate those needs. As green building philosophies continue to emerge

The Lentz House restored by Kinsley Construction featuring historically replicated windows by Marvin Windows and Doors.

as a key component in creating truly successful building projects in the region, LightStyles plans to keep pace by expanding its distribution of products with viable green solutions.

LightStyles product expansion already has included the addition of Integrity Windows and Doors from Marvin, and Infinity Replacement Windows and Doors from Marvin. These products are made of fiberglass—a material that outperforms and outlasts other materials made with petroleum, a key element in vinyl.

Grothey Farm House restored by Kinsley Construction featuring historically replicated windows by Marvin Windows and Doors.

Knowing that the people of LightStyles are who make the company perform at its best, Bob has expanded its educational department to better serve each person in its supply chain—providing educational training and access to experts so that its entire operation runs at optimum efficiency for suppliers, retailers and customers. LightStyles moves confidently into the future, shedding light on future generations, one window and door at a time.

MID PENN BANK

For 140 years, the employees of Mid Penn Bank have been serving the communities that they call home, through branches in Cumberland, Dauphin, Northumberland and Schuylkill counties. With a legacy of giving back to the residents and communities that make the bank's operation viable, Mid Penn Bank returns that trust by investing in and supporting efforts that keep the local communities it serves vibrant, staying true to its promise of "Making things happen for you."

In the wake of the Civil War, a bank was opened in Millersburg, Pennsylvania, at 349 Union Street, a location that still serves as the bank's headquarters to this day. At that time, the then-named Millersburg Bank had four employees and assets totaling $16,000. For almost a hundred years, this bank would serve only the Millersburg community. However, in 1962 the bank began expanding its service area by adding a second branch in Elizabethville through a merger with the neighboring Lykens Valley Bank.

Millersburg Bank, circa 1927.

By the time the bank celebrated its centennial in 1968, it employed 60 people and had assets of close to $30 million. Another merger occurred in 1971, when the institution was re-christened Mid Penn Bank. The 1990s represented a time of unparalleled growth, when branches were opened in Harrisburg, Halifax, Dauphin and Mechanicsburg. The bank, which debuted on the New York Stock Exchange in 1997, has continued its growth into the 21st century, now employing 160 and with assets totaling more than $572 million, and its current listing on the prestigious NASDAQ exchange (MPB). It is this consistent success, as well as the bank's staunch commitment to the communities it serves, that has placed Mid Penn Bank in *U.S. Banker* magazine's list of the nation's 200 top-performing community banks time and again.

Mid Penn Bank's community ties extend both to the manner in which the bank is managed as well as its outreach efforts. First and foremost, the company has remained committed to maintaining local management in order to best serve its customers. The bank is both headquartered and managed locally, with only local residents and/or business owners serving as board members and advisory board members. Daily operations are also community-based, with all branch offices and support functions on site in Pennsylvania; deposits and loans are all deployed to local residents through a branch network where the branch managers are integrated into the activities and development of those communities. Additionally, the various branches employ area

A recent photo of the Millersburg branch, their first office and headquarters.

residents. In turn, these bank staff members serve on local organizations that invest in and cater to local communities.

The bank also makes a concerted effort to contribute and revitalize its resident communities. Donations and sponsorships from the bank go to support local economic development, education, arts and human services improvements for area residents. The bank also underwrites charity events throughout the region with thousands of dollars worth of support.

Another method of encouraging local altruism and community spirit is through the bank's annual Everyday Heroes program, in which non-profit organizations are asked to nominate local residents who are making a difference in the community. Out of approximately 50 to 75 nominees, four are honored at a special banquet and given $1,000 to donate to the charity of their choice.

Another example of the strong ties between the bank and the community comes from the story of Mr. Allen Gilbert, who became president of Mid Penn Bank in 1931, the third generation in his family to fill that role. Though Mr. Gilbert passed away in 1955, his legacy of giving remains through the stewardship of the bank. Mid Penn remains trustee of his trust fund, which goes partly to a scholarship for local graduating seniors and partly for entertainment of the young people in the community.

In addition to the formal sponsorships and donations that the bank makes to community organizations, it also supports employees' efforts to volunteer and conduct fundraisers. For example, after a recent home fire in Millersburg, employees conducted a "casual day" fundraiser to help the resident, with the bank matching all donations made by employees. In these meaningful ways, Mid Penn Bank and its employees make a difference every day.

But none of this success would be possible without competitive financial products and excellent customer service, hallmarks of Mid Penn Bank since its inception. The bank offers a full array of financial services at its 14 branches, from personal banking to business accounts, along with comprehensive loan services for consumers, businesses and homeowners and a full-service trust and wealth management department.

Mid Penn Bank also has always offered the latest in services and products to its customers. In 1971, the bank installed a new, state-of-the-art technology: an ATM machine. Dubbed "Penny the Anytime Teller," this was just one of many advancements Mid Penn Bank would introduce through the years. Mid Penn

Allentown Blvd. branch.

introduced its "interactive branch" Web site in 2000 and continues to provide technology solutions for its customers such as Deposit XPRE$$, launched in 2008, which allows business owners to run deposits on-site.

Mid Penn Bank has excelled in its role as an independent local establishment, with continued growth and success all the while holding to its traditional ideals. "The world has changed greatly since Millersburg Bank first opened for business, and we've kept pace with it," said Kevin Laudenslager, Northern region president and COO, "But what Mid Penn Bank has never changed since that first day is our commitment to local banking."

Given this winning formula, it seems sure the bank will remain a cornerstone of Pennsylvania communities for generations to come.

PLOUSE PRECISION MANUFACTURING, INC.

With more than a half century of experience stamping, turning, grinding and milling materials from steel to plastic, Plouse Precision Manufacturing, Inc. has earned a stellar reputation for producing high-quality parts and assemblies for companies throughout North America. The company's success can be traced to founder John Plouse, whose flare for industrial design was bolstered by a demanding and customer-based work ethic. Always focused on delivering quality work at competitive prices, today the company, which celebrated 50 years of business in 2007, is a fixture in the Harrisburg, Pennsylvania-area machining industry.

As a child of the Great Depression, John Plouse wanted to learn a solid trade that would guarantee him a lifetime of employment. He enrolled in Hershey Vocational School in Hershey, Pa., where he discovered that working with precision tools appealed to his exacting nature and his knack for creative problem solving. He went on to found Plouse Machine Shop in his garage in 1957.

Over the decades, Plouse has evolved into a full-service manufacturing company that has produced everything from petals for copper roses to medical equipment and from circuit breaker components to parts for coin wrapping machines.

While John Plouse passed away in 1997, the company continues as Plouse Precision Manufacturing, a name change made in 2008 to better describe just what the company does. Today long-time employee Kermit Seitz is the CEO of the company and his son, Dale Seitz, serves as president. In 1965 when Kermit Seitz, then a jet mechanic at Olmstead Airforce Base in Middletown, Pa., joined the company, it had grown to include 20 skilled machinists. "When they closed Olmstead, I was out of a job," says Kermit. "John hired me and we hit it off pretty well. I lived right down the street and walked to work every day for the next 34 years."

Kermit's memories help keep John's legacy alive in the company. "John was

Dale and Kermit Seitz receive a state legislative proclamation for the business at their 2008 open house.

an excellent mechanic and a great idea man," he recalls. " He thrived on design challenges." John Plouse's talent for innovation was noticed at every company he worked at prior to starting his own business, and these former employers eventually became valued customers when he ventured out on his own.

His initial operation consisted of several machines in the garage of his home on Pine Hill Road in Hummelstown, where he began designing and building dies for a manufacturing company in nearby Mount Joy. Plouse's customers used these specialized tools to cut, shape and form a wide variety of products and components. Soon one of his former employers, AMP, a manufacturer of electronic connectors, approached John Plouse about making a prototype for a crimper, which is a tool that crimps terminals on the ends of wires. "His relationship with AMP really blossomed," says Kermit Seitz, "and we did a lot of business together over the years."

Within two years of starting his business, John Plouse outgrew his garage and built a small shop across the street from his house. With the business growing, Kermit Seitz was asked to use his skills in the office where he did the purchasing, scheduling and pricing. Over the next

20 years, he saw the building across from John Plouse's home expand several times.

By the 1980s, the computer revolution hit the machining industry. Initially, John Plouse resisted computerization. However, the company he founded was able to make the transition as a result of the strong foundation he had fashioned and the staff's commitment to continuously developing new and better methods for meeting customers' needs.

Part of this strong foundation was arranging for Kermit Seitz and fellow employees, David Smith and Richard Bertolette, to become partners in the business and take over its ownership after John Plouse's death. The company remains privately owned, with Kermit Seitz, Dale Seitz, Dave Smith, Jeff Bertolette and Darryl Smith as partners. Richard Bertolette retired in April of 2008.

Kermit's son, Dale, joined the company in 1998. With 15 years of plant management experience, he has a strong background in accounting and, just as important, computer information systems. He got right to work on more fully integrating the computer systems into the manufacturing process. "We went from two or three computers to more than 35 today," says Dale Seitz. "Most of the machines are computer controlled and are programmed from the computer-assisted design drawings that the customer supplies or that we engineer based on the customer's needs."

By 1999, Plouse was ready to expand again moving from its original location on Pine Hill Road to 4510 Paxton St. in Harrisburg. The operation occupied 11,000 of the 23,000-square-foot cement-block warehouse and the remainder was leased. Plouse remained in the Harrisburg area for a variety of reasons, including the strong work ethic of the area's labor force and the region's proximity to major manufacturers and metropolitan areas, such as Philadelphia, New York and Baltimore. Harrisburg's network of interstates and its airport also make transportation of raw materials and finished products logistically attractive.

At the same time the company was moving into its new building, Plouse management began to reconsider its heavy reliance on one customer: AMP. This was brought home in dollars and cents when AMP, which had been acquired by TYCO International, had its operations downsized considerably. Plouse responded quickly by making development of new business across diverse industries a top company priority. Acknowledging that sales and marketing don't always come naturally to people who operate machines, management brought in an expert—Karl Fisher, a telephone prospector, who hit the phones hard. "He was very effective at getting his foot in the door of these companies," Dale Seitz recalls.

As new business came in, Fisher, and a growing staff of sales professionals and estimators, continued exploring new industries to keep the customer base as

Wire EDM machine being shown on a group tour at their 2007 open house.

diversified as possible. This was supported by Plouse's investment in new equipment and technology, making them more desirable as a supplier to their potential customers. By the time the recession of 2001 took hold, Plouse was able to weather the storm without layoffs, although those were tough times during that period.

Today, Plouse serves seven different industries: aerospace, automotive, defense, electronics and semiconductors, food and beverage, medical and original equipment manufacturers (OEMs). "Thanks to an influx of new work from various industries, we have doubled the size of our company in just two years," says Dale Seitz. Plouse now occupies 100 percent of the space in its Harrisburg facility and has kept work flowing through the economic downturn that began in 2008, thanks to its marketing strategy and customer commitment. "Typically when one company is having an off year, another is having a pretty good one," he says. "Our sales department researches which industries are having a strong year and pursues them as perspective customers."

Plouse has also remained on the leading edge of technology, recently adding a horizontal computerized numerical controller (CNC) milling machine as part of their integrated system. This combination creates a cell that reduces "idle" time in the manufacturing process. Across the facility is the CNC-controlled

wire electrical discharge machining (EDM), which can be programmed with complex geometries to produce precision parts to a high level of accuracy. Wire EDM is a non-traditional method of removing material by a series of rapidly recurring electrical arcing discharges between an electrode (the wire) and the work piece.

Globalization is another force that Plouse has learned to contend with over the last decade as a growing portion of the machining business moves overseas. "We can be very competitive in the area of prototypes," says Dale Seitz. "We really excel when a company needs a quick turnaround time to get a new product to market. You don't see that going overseas." Looking forward, Plouse is trying to anticipate and prepare for tomorrow's business challenges. Possibly the biggest, will be recruiting a new generation of young machinists. With most schools gearing their programs to four-year colleges, the number of students in technical fields has dropped dramatically. "We have a reasonably stable workforce right now," says Dale Seitz, "but we're always looking for experienced people."

Understanding the importance of technical education, not only to their business but also to the region, business partner and sales manager David Smith is on the Advisory Committee of the Dauphin County Technical School, where he helps to strengthen its vocational-technical program. Plouse also sponsors the Palmyra Area High School FIRST Robotics Team 2539, assisting with manufacturing parts for their robot used at an annual competition.

In its more than 50 years, Plouse has continually grown to match the changing world of machining; evolving from manually operated lathes and mills to the latest in CNC horizontal and vertical machining centers. With a continuing commitment to innovation, precision, customer service and quality, Plouse continues to be on the leading edge in manufacturing in Harrisburg and around the country. For more information, go to www.PlouseManufacturing.com

PREMIER EYE CARE GROUP

Premier Eye Care Group started caring for patients on April 15, 1981. Jane Barton, M.D., opened the practice in Harrisburg, Pennsylvania, locating it in the historic district of Shipoke. She shared space with Dr. Ed Steele, a general surgeon, in the building that was then known as the Steele Medical Building. In the beginning the practice name was Ophthalmology, A Professional Corporation. Dr. Barton had received a B.S. degree from the University of Nebraska in Lincoln, earned an M.D. from the Medical College of Pennsylvania, completed a rotating internship at Harrisburg Hospital, and completed an ophthalmology residency at Wills Eye Hospital in Philadelphia. Following her residency, she worked with Dr. Turgot Hamdi, a pioneer in intraocular lens implantation. For a few months she also worked in the office of Dr. Charles Rife.

Dr. Barton performed the first corneal transplant at The Harrisburg Hospital, and was the first eye surgeon in the area to use topical anesthesia (no needle) for cataract surgery. An active member of the teaching staff at Wills Eye for a decade after her training, she served as Chief of Ophthalmology at Harrisburg Hospital for more than ten years. Dr. Barton brought the phaco-emulsification procedure for cataract surgery to Harrisburg.

Dr. Jane Barton with one of her first patients in April 1981.

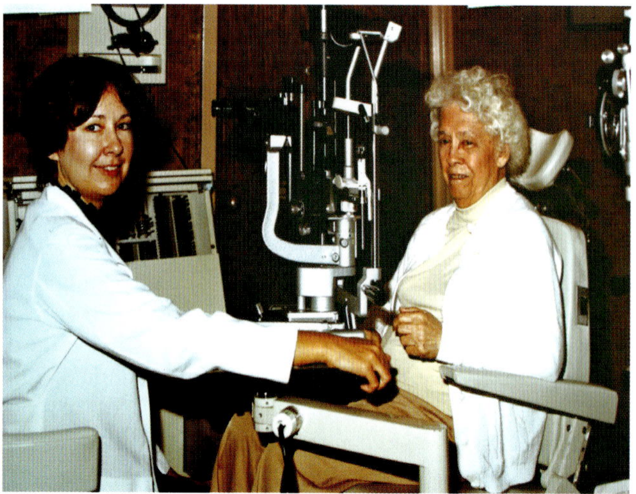

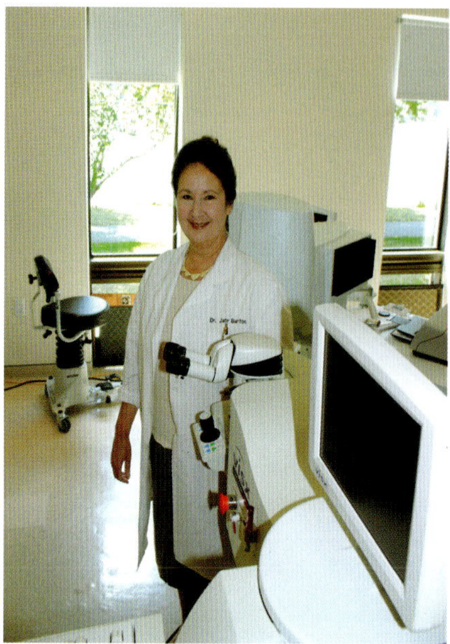

Dr. Jane Barton with their new excimer laser, summer 2008.

This is a modern form of cataract surgery in which the eye's internal lens is emulsified with ultrasound and aspirated from the eye, then replaced with an intra-ocular lens implant.

Active in the community, Dr. Barton has served as president of the Dauphin County Medical Society and president of the Pennsylvania Academy of Ophthalmology. She was a member of Pennsylvania's Health Care Cost Containment Council. She is certified by the American Board of Ophthalmology and is a Fellow of the American College of Surgeons. Dr. Barton is married to Michael Barton, Ph.D., Professor of American Studies and Social Science at Penn State University at Harrisburg and author of this book. They have a son in medical school and a daughter who graduated from Harvard Law School and is practicing law in Philadelphia.

In 1986, Dr. Barton was joined by Dr. Robert Mandel, who also had received his ophthalmology training at Wills Eye Hospital where he had served as chief resident. During the time Dr. Mandel was with the practice he also served on the teaching staff at Wills Eye Hospital, and he pursued and received an MBA degree from the Wharton School of Business at the University of Pennsylvania. In 1993, Dr. Mandel was involved in the negotiations for Premier Eye Care Group to purchase Dr. Peter Anker's ophthalmology practice, which was located in a building that Dr. Anker had built on North Front Street in Harrisburg. John O'Donnell, O.D., joined the practice about this time. He started referring to the practice as "the premier eye care group in central Pennsylvania," and soon the name Premier Eye Care Group, Inc. officially was adopted. Dr. Mandel joined the management of Pinnacle Health System, but continued to practice ophthalmology part time with Premier. Dr. Mandel eventually accepted the position as medical director for Massachusetts Blue Shield insurance company, and moved out of state.

The Premier Laser and Surgical Center was opened in the spring of 1994. This gave the practice more opportunity to adopt and keep up with the best in procedures and equipment for the surgical treatment of eye disease, including the life-enhancing LASIK procedures.

In 2000, Premier Eye Care Group was privileged to purchase the practice and assume care of Dr. Robert Shindler's patients. Dr. Shindler (also Wills Eye trained) was a respected eye doctor in the community. This office is located on Cedar Cliff Drive in Camp Hill, giving Premier Eye Care Group a location on the west shore.

Geoffrey J. Brent, M.D., joined the practice in 1996 and is now a partner. He is a board-certified ophthalmologist trained at the prestigious Cleveland Clinic Foundation. He provides a full range of medical and surgical treatments for eye disease and offers LASIK and other refractive surgical procedures to reduce the dependence on eyeglasses and contact lenses. Today, Premier Eye Group's practitioners provide seminars on LASIK and other vision correction procedures such as implantable lenses and conductive keratoplasty (a non-invasive procedure for treating farsightedness) and presbyopia (a process that reduces the need for bifocals). These seminars offer patients the opportunity to meet Premier Eye Care doctors and pose any questions they may have about eye care.

Dr. Barton and Dr. Brent have performed thousands of refractive surgery procedures in Premier Eye Care's Ophthalmology Laser & Surgery Center. Premier Eye Care Group is one of the few practices nationwide that tracks patient outcomes on a regular basis and confidently publishes these outcomes on the company's Web site, premiereyes.com.

Premier Eye Care offers LASIK, cataract surgery and other procedures that can improve a patient's vision or reduce a patient's dependency on glasses or contacts. The procedures that are possible these days keep Dr. Barton and Dr. Brent moving forward at a steady pace. For

Dr. Geoffrey Brent in their LASIK Suite, summer 2008.

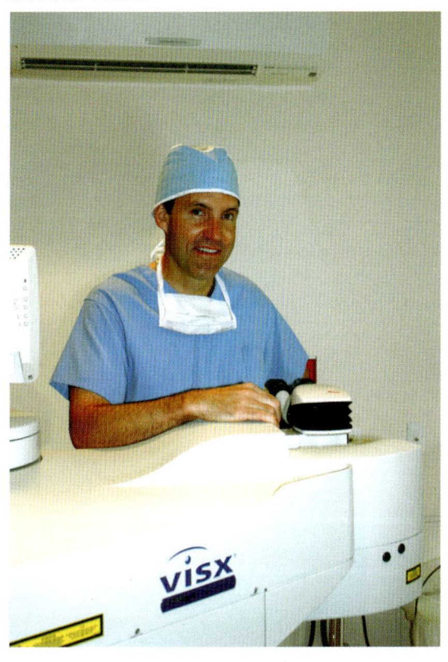

Premier Eye Care Group offices at 2745 North Front Street, Harrisburg, Pennsylvania.

example, Keratoconus, a disease of the cornea, can be treated with INTACS, microscopic segments inserted into the cornea to stabilize and improve the clarity of refraction. Also, they offer implantable lenses that do not require the removal of the natural lens for those patients who are not candidates for LASIK because of especially high eyeglass prescriptions or thin corneas. The practice is, in fact, the only one in central Pennsylvania to offer all FDA-certified refractive procedures to better serve the individual.

The Surgery Center continues to upgrade equipment and methods and currently offers what we believe are the two best excimer lasers in the world for LASIK. The Visx Star 4 IR (iris registration) with Advanced Customvue is the laser that has been used to increase contrast sensitivity for some U.S. Navy pilots and has been dubbed iLASIK by AMO (the company that makes the Star 4 IR). The iLASIK procedure includes the use of the 60 hertz Intralase laser to make the flap and the Advanced CustomVue WaveScan to create a customized treatment, which Premier does. The other laser is the Allegretto Wave Eye-Q 400 hertz excimer, the fastest excimer laser available today. It individu-

alizes the treatment to account for the different curvatures of a patient's eye. These lasers work phenomenally well, maximizing safety and results. The choice of laser is prescribed according to a patient's particular measurements and needs.

Premier's staff currently totals more than 80 employees. A number of them have been with the organization for 20 years or more. Most of the ophthalmic assistants are certified. Anne Quist, who has been with Premier for 10 years, calls it a "family-friendly place." Premier also is working on being more online-friendly, providing a way to sign up for seminars. Premier Eye Care Group is ordering prescriptions online and embracing methods that help cut down on healthcare cost and errors.

Premier's service as well as equipment is state-of-the-art. Premier Eye Care Group offers doctor availability for emergencies seven days a week, 24 hours per day. The practice provides comprehensive eye care to all of Central Pennsylvania and is proud of its professional staff that provides the most advanced methods of eye care diagnosis and treatment.

PRL, INC.

PRL, Inc. is located in Cornwall, Pennsylvania, a small town whose rich history of iron and industry stretches back to the mid-1700s. The company is located next to Cornwall Furnace, which operated as a foundry from 1742 until 1883, and supplied munitions during the Revolutionary War. Today it is a historical museum. PRL, Inc. continues the area's long-standing industrial tradition by supplying high specification metal components and services to a variety of markets, including energy and defense.

The founder of Pennsylvania Radiographic Laboratories (PRL), Benjamin Chase, worked for Lebanon Steel Foundry as a Production Manager. During his time, Chase noticed that castings tended to pile up in the Radiography Department, where they were sent to be x-rayed for defects. He determined that a company specializing in Radiography could relieve the bottleneck and be successful. In 1969, Chase decided to pursue his idea and the next year he opened Pennsylvania Radiographic Laboratories. He was joined in the enterprise by two of his coworkers, Larry Heffner and Robert Wagner, who worked for PRL until their retirement, and his friend L. Saylor Zimmerman, III, who is currently PRL's Vice President of Finance.

Sadly, Chase never had the opportunity to witness the success of his idea. He passed away unexpectedly while on vacation in St. Maarten in 1971. This tragic event might have signaled the end of the company, but according to Zimmerman the company operated on a "wing and a prayer" until it was purchased by Erwin "Herk" Herschkowitz a year later.

Austrian by birth, Herschkowitz had moved with his parents to Tarija, Bolivia in 1938. He graduated from high school there and pursued a Bachelor's degree in Civil Engineering from the University of Louisville, followed by a second degree in Petroleum Engineering from Penn State University.

Mining in the iron ore pit (next to PRL's current location) in 1880.

There he met Barbara Lightner, a native of Western Pennsylvania. After their graduation, they were married and moved to Bolivia, where Herk worked for YPFB, the government-owned oil company.

After four years with the company, Herschkowitz took a job with a Bolivian construction company, where he worked as General Manager. The main projects were U. S. Government funded, including the expansion of the La Paz airport. By 1971, political unrest in Bolivia had reached threatening levels, and the Herschkowitz family, which now included two daughters, reluctantly moved to the United States. With an uncertain future, Herk learned about the availability of Pennsylvania Radiographic Laboratories from a college fraternity brother, Charles Brooks, Jr.

Still in its infancy, PRL had only 15 employees at that time, and its facilities were located in a rented building in Lebanon, Pennsylvania. Fortunately, Herschkowitz was able to draw on his vast work experience and managerial skills, and within the next decade he changed the name of the company to PRL, Inc., relocated it to Cornwall, Pennsylvania, expanded the capabilities, added a metallurgical lab, and improved the company's Quality Assurance System, which became ASME Certified. In 1977, he purchased Brenner Machine Company, which was founded in 1916 and located in Myerstown, where it was operated by the Brenner family

PRL's management team in 1987.

Jan Herschkowitz (PRL, Inc.'s President since 1989) with a portrait of her father "Herk" (President from 1972 to 1989).

until 1960. In order to further diversify, in 1985, Herschkowitz also acquired Lebanon Tool Company (LTC, Inc.), another machine shop known as "The Home of Precision", from Jack Sherman who had started the company in 1953.

PRL, Inc., which is still owned by the Herschkowitz family, was established as a holding company in 1985. Today, its three operating subsidiaries provide complete turnkey capabilities for high specification castings in the defense, energy and commercial markets. PRL Industries, Inc. upgrades castings utilizing a wide range of Non-Destructive Examination (NDE) techniques in accordance to required procedures. Brenner Machine Company was merged into LTC, Inc. in 2007. The Cornwall location specializes in machining on larger metal components of up to 10,000 pounds, while the Lebanon plant focuses on CNC machining larger quantities of smaller parts, down to a tolerance of 1/100,000th of an inch. Completing the PRL family is Regal Cast, Inc. which was opened in 1989 as a ferrous and non-ferrous foundry and pours sand castings ranging in weight from two pounds to 4 tons.

Herk's daughter Patricia joined the company in 1985 as Director of Public Relations. Through PRL she became active in the Submarine Industrial Base Council where she currently serves as Pennsylvania's Co-chair.

Given the nature of PRL's work, its company has often paralleled the history of the nuclear and defense industries in the United States—for better and for worse. In the 1970s, PRL gained a nationwide reputation as a supplier of castings used in valves, pumps, and turbines for the nuclear power industry. In 1979, the accident that occurred at Three Mile Island led to an eventual moratorium on nuclear power plant construction.

Due to the incident, the demand for castings to be used in nuclear facilities fell sharply, and PRL had to find a new market for its services. The company re-diversified and became a defense contractor, which for the remainder of the Cold War was the primary source of PRL's business. During this period,

One of Regal Cast's first pours in 1989 at PRL's then recently established foundry, Regal Cast, Inc.

PRL grew rapidly. In 1988, after a bout with cancer, Herschkowitz asked his daughter Janis to join him in the business. At the time, she was working in the Chicago area as Financial Manager of a $185 million Division of Zenith Electronics Corporation. Unfortunately father and daughter worked together for only seven weeks when Herk's cancer returned, and several months later he passed away. It was a difficult time.

Prior to his death, Herschkowitz felt that PRL would be unable to survive without a foundry. The industry was becoming increasingly cut throat and PRL found itself competing with its own suppliers. Under Jan's direction his dream became a reality. Although he never set foot in the foundry, he did know Jan had secured financing before he died.

The foundry had to be operational quickly, because as soon as its existence was known, PRL's casting supplier base would be jeopardized. Thus an empty building was secured, and within three months of signing the bank papers, Regal Cast poured its first casting.

According to Jan Herschkowitz, "It was an amazing team effort. Permits had to be obtained and new electrical services, furnaces, cranes, ladle heaters, and sand and dust collection systems had to be ordered and installed. At one point, we had five outside sub-contractors working with our internal maintenance crew. In retrospect, I don't know how we did it."

When the Berlin Wall fell, PRL was once again severely impacted. "Four years later," as Herschkowitz recalls, "we were very close to closing our doors. We were highly leveraged due to the start up of Regal Cast, and we lost 80% of our customer base. PRL managed to survive due to sheer determination, a highly skilled work force, a dedicated management team, a fear of failure and dumb luck." According to Herschkowitz, "The hardest part was cutting costs. The worst feeling in the world is walking through a shop after you have reduced your work force."

It was an extremely difficult time for the company, which went from a high of 222 employees in 1990 to a low of 106 in 1993. During this tumultuous period, Jan says business was touch-and-go. "We had no time to develop a master plan," she said, laughing at how far that ideal was from the reality. "We would just sit down in a conference room and collectively figure out how we were going to get through the week!"

Both father and daughter attribute the success of PRL, Inc. to its outstanding employees. Upon being awarded Small Business of the Year by the Lebanon County Chamber of Commerce in 1988, Mr. Herschkowitz gave full credit to his co-workers. When Jan was recognized as one of the Best Fifty Business Women in Pennsylvania in 1997, she attributed her success in the industry to her male dominated team.

Despite the challenges faced at work, Herschkowitz has also found the time to become active in the community by serving on various local boards. In 1992 she was Chairman of the Lebanon Valley Chamber of Commerce. She also was appointed as a delegate to the White House conference on Small business in 1995, served on Governor Ridge's transition team as a member of the study group for Labor and Industry, and was Chairman of the Business Advisory Council for the Federal Reserve Bank of Philadelphia. Currently, Herschkowitz is a member of the Board of Directors of Mutual Benefit Group, an insurance company, as well as the Pennsylvania Chamber of Commerce.

Through her involvement in the community, Herschkowitz found herself gravitating towards politics. According to Jan, "I was becoming increasingly frustrated with the negative impact Government policies were having on small manufacturers, so I became more active in the National

Inspection Department at PRL.

Federation of Independent Business (NFIB), and started contacting my legislators on a regular basis!" Her voice was not unheard and in 2004 she received the opportunity of a lifetime when she was invited with other business leaders to brief President Bush at the White House. Three years later, Jan successfully underwent a U.S. Senate confirmation hearing, and received a Presidential Appointment for the Board of Directors of the National Consumer co-operative Bank.

Realizing the important role PRL plays in our nation's defense and in the community various politicians have visited the company, including Vice President Cheney, Senator Specter, Senator Santorum, Congressman Gekas, Congressman Holden and numerous state legislators. Jan's activism has not gone unnoticed and in 2007 she received an NFIB award as "Pennsylvania's Small Business Champion of the Year." She remains active with NFIB and currently serves as Chairman of the Pennsylvania Leadership Safe Trust. According to Jan, "I will continue to be a vocal advocate for small business since it is companies such as PRL that are the engine that runs our economy. We need the government to help us, not hinder us."

Today PRL is a thriving company thanks to their employees and, as Zimmerman says "the leadership of Jan and her father." Currently, with 150 employees, PRL Inc. has found an increase in nuclear energy work, as the operating licenses of existing plants are being extended, and defense work continues to be strong, particularly in the nuclear submarine sector. With new prospects on the horizon and an outstanding team behind her Jan says, "Although there are always challenges, our future has never been brighter."

Vice President and Mrs. Dick Cheney during their 2004 Visit to PRL. Photo by Bill Simone

MCNEES WALLACE & NURICK LLC

Established in 1935, McNees Wallace & Nurick LLC (McNees) has played a major role in the legal and community life of Harrisburg and central Pennsylvania. In 2010 when the law firm celebrates its 75th anniversary, twelve special charities are going to celebrate with them. "Each month we will choose one charitable or civic activity and contribute an extraordinary level of service, tying it into our 75th anniversary," says David M. Kleppinger, the firm's Chairman. "For example, one of our attorneys serves on the board of the local Habitat for Humanity, and another is a member on the United Way board, so we'll designate a month to provide additional personnel or resources to those organizations."

The anniversary would no doubt please the firm's founder, Sterling G. McNees, a graduate of the University of Pittsburgh Law School. He became a circuit-riding lawyer in his home region before coming to Harrisburg in 1920 as a temporary assistant to the superintendent of public instruction. The following year he was appointed a deputy attorney general of Pennsylvania, and three years later moved to Harrisburg permanently and entered private law practice.

The practice was very successful and in 1931 McNees employed Gilbert Nurick, a recent graduate of Dickinson School of Law, as an associate. An early advocate of strengthening bar disciplinary procedures, Nurick is respected throughout the country for his work in this field. David M. Wallace, a graduate of Dickinson School of Law, and a veteran of the American Expeditionary Force in France during World War I, joined the firm in 1942 giving the firm its current name. While the founders have long since passed away, the law firm they created continues to carry their names and is enjoying considerable success in both law and public service.

The last quarter century have been years of remarkable growth and maturity for the firm.

"Twenty-five years ago we were a single-office firm in Harrisburg," says Kleppinger. "Today we have expanded geographically to Columbus, Ohio, and Washington, DC, and in Pennsylvania we have offices in State College, Lancaster and Hazleton. The headquarters remains in Harrisburg." During that period the firm has grown from 45 lawyers to 127

supported by 22 paraprofessionals and an administrative staff of 109. Today, McNees is a full-service business and corporate law firm that services the needs of small to large businesses as well as sole proprietorships and individuals.

"One area we didn't have 25 years ago that we are quite active in now is intellectual property," says Kleppinger. McNees now has a substantial patent, trademark and copyright practice with a dozen patent lawyers. Another area of expansion is the firm's practice before the Public Utility Commissions in Pennsylvania, Ohio, and several other states. "We've been in the forefront of the restructuring and partial deregulation of utility services including telecommunications, electricity and natural gas, from both a legislative and a regulatory perspective," says Kleppinger.

McNees attorneys have always been active at various levels in the Dauphin County Bar Association. McNees founder Gilbert Nurick served a term as President and current attorney James P. DeAngelo will be President during the firm's 75th anniversary year in 2010.

Community involvement is deeply woven into the firm's cultural fabric. All attorneys are encouraged to donate pro bono services, which they provide individually and through Central Pennsylvania Legal Services. The firm lists over 200 charitable and community groups it has assisted and boards on which its lawyers have served. So important is community service to McNees that it seems natural that the firm is dedicating its 75th anniversary year to activities that will profoundly and positively impact the community for years to come.

Sterling G. McNees.

Gilbert Nurick.

THE WARRELL CORPORATION

Sweet dreams, delicious candies and the well-seasoned business acumen of Lincoln Warrell, chairman of the Warrell Corporation, have created sweet success for the Camp Hill, Pennsylvania-based candy manufacturing company. The family-owned business, which began in 1957, was purchased in 1965 by the Warrell family. Pennsylvania Dutch Candies and later Katharine Beecher Candies are the brands that the company produces, along with creating an ever-growing number of candies and snack items for contract manufacturing and packaging for private labels. The multimillion-dollar company has grown steadily and is now more than fifty times its original size, but its beginnings are as homespun as family.

Carrol Warrell, Lincoln's brother, always dreamed that his brother and father, Jonas, would break free of employment to others and start their own family business. Lincoln Warrell, a graduate of Penn State with a chemical engineering degree, was working for the Aluminum Company of America (Alcoa) at the time. Carrol began researching companies and happened upon Pennsylvania Dutch Candies, a small manufacturer of nostalgic candies

Lincoln Warrell, chairman of The Warrell Corporation after receiving the prestigious Candy Industry's Kettle Award.

and fancy food items located in the quaint, historic town of Mt. Holly Springs.

The brothers, along with their father, then president of Carlisle Tire and Rubber Co., a Carlisle Corporation, pooled their money and bought the fledgling company. None of the Warrell family had any direct experience in the candy business, but Lincoln Warrell had a strong incentive and a great attitude to make it work. "At Alcoa, I had one of the top five sales jobs in the country," Warrell says. "With five children and entering an unknown business with sales of less than a million dollars and no profits to that date

—well, I like challenges and that certainly was a good one."

Warrell was ready for any challenge, and on his first day as owner of the company, he was faced with an interesting one. Warrell's quick, can-do attitude demonstrated he was willing to roll up his sleeves and get to work. "They brought up an old, dirty wooden desk, which had been in storage, and placed it

1960 Promotion of Pennsylvania Dutch Candies' honey, jams and jellies at 1 of 36 Hough Baking Stores in Cleveland Ohio.

1966 Feature Dept. in the gourmet food section of B. Altman & Co. in New York City.

in a shared office for me. Well, the first thing I did was to get some soap and water and clean that desk. Then I was put in charge of purchasing janitorial supplies for the company, something I also knew nothing about."

One thing Warrell did know about was sales. Having been his area of expertise in his previous career, he knew the best resource to generate new business was through current customers. Pennsylvania Dutch's existing customers were family-owned gift shops, old country stores, roadside stands and retail areas in restaurants, amusement parks and caverns. They carried items such as greeting cards, gift baskets, plush animals and nostalgic candy and snack items from Pennsylvania Dutch. Warrell went on the road and visited his customers to hear their opinions of the company and specifically what areas needed to be addressed. Warrell recalls, "I received an earful on those visits, with several brokers telling me how disgruntled they were with the company's performance as a supplier. Their complaints ranged from slow pay to late delivery." Warrell addressed those issues and within a year,

Modern 42 inch chocolate enrober coating pretzels.

Remodeled 200,000 square-foot plant in Camp Hill, Pennsylvania.

the company's sales doubled. Unfortunately, Pennsylvania Dutch Candy (PDC) still showed little profit. It was then when Warrell made one of many bold decisions to come. He increased the retail price 25 percent in order to improve the retailers' and his profitability. PDC took 4 percent and their customers received 21 percent, which proved successful.

Warrell always was open to creative, new ways to market the business. He realized that the size of the Mt. Holly plant was ideal for plant tours. He added an antique bike museum and opened the plant for free tours. Since that first tour, thousands of people have enjoyed, and today fondly remember, seeing chocolate candies being made at the Mt. Holly Pennsylvania Dutch Plant.

In addition to his innovative marketing initiatives, Warrell had ideas about how to improve production. His willingness to learn all aspects of the candy-making processes served his company well. He patiently absorbed the candy-making methods already in place. He then, respectfully, but boldly, challenged some of those very processes.

Katharine Beecher, which the company acquired in 1974, was primarily a butter mint candy manufacturer and distributor. The quality was superb, but the customer base was not large enough to contribute to the company's overall growth. Warrell purchased butter toasting nut equipment from a friend for $3,500. He then added his originality to a process known as hot-panning. By adding a sugar solution to this precise method of slow coating nut meat-based

items, Warrell had an end product of goodies such as butter or honey toasted peanuts, cashews and pecans. This process opened up the product line and increased Katherine Beecher's sales. The new line of products helped grow the Warrell Corporation's overall customer base, which served an increasing number of contract manufacturing customers. The company now has 22 gas-fired copper kettles, making it one of the largest hot-panning operations in the country.

In 1982 the company acquired Melster Candies, which made a variety of marshmallow products including circus peanuts. The company was located in Cambridge, Wisconsin and only produced circus peanuts in the winter months due to the poor drying process. When Warrell investigated the system more carefully, he quickly found a way to increase production. "They told me that we couldn't make circus peanuts year-round because of the heat and humidity present during the summer," states Warrell. "Well, when you have a window open in what was then the drying room, it becomes obvious why you couldn't. We added a controlled air conditioning and dehumidification system as well as built proper drying rooms and began making circus peanuts year-round." After several years, Melster became the nation's largest supplier of circus peanuts.

Warrell found that there were many 'old wives' tales' and thoughts about what could and could not be done in the candy-making business. He applied his straight-forward logic, dispelled other antiquated processes and began approaching manufacturing in fresh, innovative ways.

Warrell made another bold move in the year 2000. He decided to consolidate the Pennsylvania Dutch Candies and Katharine Beecher Candies production facilities into a 200,000 square-foot processing facility. The new candy plant is located in Camp Hill, Pennsylvania. Although reluctant at first, Warrell determined that retrofitting the old facility to the specifications needed for the Warrell Corporation was the best move. Building renovations cost about $11 million, rather than the $30 to35 million it would have cost to build a new facility. "We're still at about half the cost of new, and some of that money is invested in new, state-of-the-art equipment," states Warrell. It took approximately one year to complete the remodeling and make the full transition into the new plant. In 2009 the facility gained a "Superior" rating from American Institute of Baking and a certification for ISO 22000 for Management Safety System.

In addition to the company's hot-panning operation are chocolate panning, which features traditional coating pans and high-capacity belt coating machines,

High speed stand-up Pouch Packing Machines.

One of many high tech packaging lines called PET.

a nut crunch line, and three enrobing lines.

Delicious results from these candy-making processes include pan-coated chocolate pecans, chocolate-covered brittle and chocolate enrobed pretzels. In addition to the company's trademark peanut brittle crunch, produced with the help of the 'nutmaster' machine, the company still makes old-fashioned peanut butter pillows made by the traditional practice of hand pulling the candy to perfect consistency and sheen.

Warrell sold Melster in 2004 to concentrate on the Pennsylvania Dutch and Katharine Beecher brands and the growing number of accounts for contract manufacturing. In addition to the two branded candy lines, The Warrell Corporation has developed long-term, contract manufacturing

partnerships with the world's top food companies. Due to confidentiality agreements, Warrell could not divulge the names of the private labels. "You've eaten a lot of our products, you just don't know it," jokes Warrell. Eighty percent of the company's production is for contract manufacturing labels while the other twenty percent is for Katherine Beecher and Pennsylvania Dutch customers.

The company now has more than 250 full-time employees working out of the Camp Hill facility. While Warrell is still an active part of the company, serving as chairman, the day-to-day operations are left to the next generation of the Warrell family and long-time friend and company president, Patrick Huffman, a well-known industry leader. Warrell's son-in-law Kevin Silva serves as vice chairman and vice president of Administration, Logistics and Warehousing. Warrell's youngest son, Richard, serves as director of Marketing and Sales of a new acquisition for the company now called Warrell Classic, formerly Classic Caramel in York, Pennsylvania. When asked what Warrell is most proud of Warrell firmly states, "I'm very proud of the people (at Warrell). I didn't do all this myself, you know that! I've been very fortunate to find good people to come aboard and work with us for over 30 years." Most helpful over the years include Richard Billman, past president, L. Robert Lebo, past secretary and treasurer, Tom Yantis, assistant secretary and treasurer and Keith Snyder, PDC shipping manager.

Good employees follow inspiring leaders, willing to take on new challenges. Warrell continues to be just that. "When I first came into the candy business, people often would ask me what I thought I possibly could contribute to the confectionery industry. I told them I was uninhibited by prior knowledge." That lack of inhibition continues to be one of the keys to the company's continued success.

PENNSYLVANIA SCHOOL BOARDS ASSOCIATION

When a group of Pennsylvania school board members met for the first time at the state capitol in Harrisburg in 1895 to address their concerns to the governor and legislators, Pennsylvania became the first state in the Union to form an association to represent the needs of local elected school officials. The article in the Harrisburg newspaper describing the formation of the Pennsylvania School Boards Association (PSBA) more than 110 years ago noted, in effect, that those local school board members were focused on the need for more state funding and fewer mandates for public schools. Tom Gentzel, PSBA's executive director, notes that it could be argued that little has changed over the years, since those remain big concerns for local school officials.

Of course, the world is much different today than in the late 19th century, and PSBA is keeping pace. Local school leaders look to the association for help complying with state laws and even federal programs, such as No Child Left Behind. "We provide workshops, publications and other assistance to help them understand what the law requires," says

Tom Gentzel, PSBA's executive director.

Gentzel. "They really look to us for that kind of support."

Still, legislative outreach is only part of the association's mission to help its member school boards become more effective. "Research shows a clear connection between how school boards conduct their business and levels of school achievement," says Gentzel. "We know that effective school boards are critical to student performance."

PSBA may be well known for the information, educational programs, legislative and legal advocacy, research, insurance programs, policy service superintendent searches and other assistance it provides to its members, but the association's top priority is helping school boards perform their vital leadership role successfully.

School board members are not paid for their service, but that does not mean their contributions are not important. "Even though it's volunteer work, serving on a school board really needs to be treated as a profession," Gentzel says. "It's more than approving a budget and making sure the buildings are maintained. The focus is on setting good policy, examining student achievement data, asking the right questions, and directing the resources to the right places. It's about making sure the district leadership is aligned with the administrative staff and the teaching staff so they're all moving in the same direction."

Gentzel describes PSBA as evolving from a traditional trade association into a professional society. The organization has developed Standards for Effective Governance and a Code of Conduct for School Board Members that lay out the expectations and best practices for school governance. More than 400 of the state's 500 school boards have adopted the standards and code, voluntarily holding themselves accountable for meeting those high expectations— and that number continues to grow. PSBA also is recognizing exemplary governance through its Master Board Member and Distinguished School Board accreditation programs.

Although PSBA helps the occasional dysfunctional school board straighten out its problems, board service usually brings out the best in people. "I've learned that those who serve on school boards typically do so for the right reasons," says Gentzel, who has been with PSBA for nearly three decades. "They care about kids and about having a good, strong school system in their community. Most importantly they understand the critical connection between a well-educated public and a strong democracy. That's why we talk about treating it as a profession."

For more information, please visit www.psba.org.

The PSBA headquarters, located in Mechanicsburg, is home to association staff who provide assistance to school boards in promoting excellence in school board governance through leadership, service and advocacy for public education.

A TIMELINE OF GREATER HARRISBURG'S HISTORY

1720s: John Harris, Sr., the pioneer, and Esther, his bride, settle on the shores of the Susquehanna river.

1728: John Harris, Jr., the future founder of Harrisburg, is baptized.

1732: Construction of Derry Presbyterian Church.

1733: Harris ferry begins operating.

1734: William Kelso's Tavern opened. The tavern became a West Shore terminal for the ferry John Harris had begun operating.

1740: Rev. John Elder builds his home. It is probably the oldest in Dauphin County. Construction of the stone Paxton Presbyterian Church.

1748: John Harris, Sr., died. He is buried by a mulberry tree beside the river in front of his home.

1751: Carlisle laid out as a town.

1755: Fort Hunter built.

1758: The first recorded flood.

1760: Tinian, the home of Colonel James Burd (1726-1798), constructed in present-day Highspire.

1761: Founding of Middletown, oldest town in Dauphin County, so named because it was between Carlisle and Lancaster.

1762: Frederick Hummel founds Hummelstown.

1763: The Paxton Boys massacre of Conestoga Indians.

1765: Thomas Lingle founds Linglestown.

1766: The home of John Harris, Jr., is completed in Harrisburg near his father's ferry station, built on ground high enough that the mansion has never been flooded.

1771: Robert Whitehill settles near what is now 19th and Market Streets in Camp Hill.

1783: Dickinson College is founded and named in honor of Governor Dickinson, who donated 700 acres of land to be sold for funds for the new college.

1784: The Great Ice Flood, March 15th. The Susquehanna crests at 25.0 feet. John Harris, Jr., starts the Harrisburg Academy. Its first class met in a room of the Harris mansion.

1785: The town of Harrisburg is laid out by William Maclay. John Harris, Jr., gave the state a tract of land as a site for a capitol. Dauphin county is created out of Lancaster county.

1787: Daniel Roberts builds a small forge and a stone house at the foot of First Mountain north of Rockville. The mile-long Conewago Canal is completed around the falls of the Susquehanna.

1789: *The Harrisburg Journal and Weekly Advertiser* appears, the first newspaper venture in Harrisburg. A post office is established in Lancaster. Residents of Harrisburg could ride there to get their mail.

1790: The first prison is built about this time on one of the lots conveyed by John Harris, Jr. William Maclay builds his mansion on Front Street. Home of the Pennsylvania Bar Association today.

1791: Six years after it was founded, Harrisburg is incorporated as a borough. The first fire company, the Union Fire Company, is organized. John Harris, Jr., dies. The Golden Sheaf tavern is built on the northwest corner of Front and Market Streets by John and Andrew Krause.

1792: A post office is established in Harrisburg, with John Montgomery as postmaster. It is located in a little room in a house on Mulberry Street. Simpson Ferry Road built. It extends from Michael Simpson's Ferry on the Susquehanna to Carlisle. Used by many for travel to the west. The *Oracle of Dauphin and Harrisburg Advertiser* newspaper is first published. Construction starts on the first courthouse—red brick, two stories high. A bison stampedes cattle into town and is shot in Harris's stable on River Street.

1793: A Yellow Fever epidemic hits the city.

1794: George Washington stops by Harrisburg. He was on his way to Carlisle to take command of the troops who would quell the Whiskey Rebellion in western Pennsylvania. Harrisburg contains 300 houses; Dauphin County's population is 18,177. The Harrisburg Library Company opens.

These riverfront mansions at Front and McClay Streets built in the late 19th Century were torn down to provide a site for the present Governor's Mansion. (HSDC)

1796: The first theater
company is organized—The
Harrisburg Company of
Comedians.

1797: The first fire engine
purchased about this time.
There was no hose, and the
bucket brigade was needed
as much as ever to supply the
water for the engine.

1798: Peace Church built
near Shiremanstown,
another religous landmark.

1801: Friendship Fire
Company organized.

1805: Gratz, across the
mountain from Lykens, is
laid out by Simon Gratz, the
"coal king."

1806: The English Presbyterian Church of Harrisburg is
erected. Before the building
was finished, the congregation worshiped outdoors
under the trees in summer, in
the courthouse, and in the
old jail.

1807: Millersburg first settled
by Daniel and John Miller.

1810: The first Methodist
congregation organized.
Previously, their ministers
were circuit riders who
traveled from one place to
another on horseback. The
first Roman Catholic congregation in Dauphin County is
organized as a mission.

1812: Harrisburg is named
the capital of Pennsylvania.
The foundation stone in the
Camelback bridge is laid.
The bridge designer is
Theodore Burr, its owner, the
Harrisburg Bridge Company.

1814: The Harrisburg Nat-
ional Bank (later Common-
wealth and now a branch of
Mellon Bank), is chartered
and opens for business.
The second oldest Fire
Company in Harrisburg, the
Hope Company, is organized.

1815: Wormleysburg laid out
by John Wormley. An
important lumbering town
on the West Shore when
Pennsylvania ranked tops in
the timber industry. The first
Zion Lutheran Church is
built near 4th and Market.

1817: Elizabethville, between
Lykens and Millersburg, is
laid out by John Bender and
named in honor of his wife.
Construction of the Camelback bridge complete. It
connects both shores. Market
Streets by way of Forster's
(now City) Island.

1818: Governor William
Findlay lays the cornerstone
for the first capitol building,
designed by Stephen Hills.

1822: The new capitol
building is completed and
ready for occupancy.
German Reformed Salem
Church—now Salem United
Church of Christ—is built at
3rd and Chesnut. It is the
oldest surviving church
building in the city. The
Zollinger hat factory, one of
the city's landmarks, is
established at 13 South
Market Square.

1824: New Bloomfield, the
county seat of Perry county,
is laid out.

1825: Three steamboats ply
the river around Harrisburg.
The following year one of
them, the *Susquehanna*
explodes, and commercial
steamboating ends.

1826: Construction of St.
Stephen's Episcopal Cathedral completed. Dauphin laid
out by Innis Green. For
many years it was known as
Greensburg; in 1845, it is
given the name of Dauphin.

1827: In the spring, 1631 rafts,
1370 arks, and about 300
keelboats pass by Harrisburg.
A branch of the German
Reformed church, the Church
of God, is founded as a
denomination in Harrisburg.
Led by the Rev. John
Winebrenner, the members
were also known as Wine-
brennarians. St. Patrick's
Cathedral is dedicated on
State Street, between Second
and Third, to serve a growing
Catholic population. The
Masonic Hall, more com-
monly called the Exchange, is
erected by Samuel Holman
on Walnut near Third.

1828: Fire destroys almost all
the buildings on the northeast side of Market Square
and the north side of Market
Street. Union Canal com-
pleted from the Schuykill
River to Middletown.

1830: The First Baptist
church in Harrisburg is
organized by seven members.
Mechanicsburg acquires its
present name.

1831: *The Harrisburg Telegraph* first published in
September. The Cumberland
Valley Railroad is incorporated but the road isn't
completed until 1841.

1833: Harrisburg Nail Works
is built in West Fairview
township on the west shore.

1834: The Pennsylvania Canal opens at Harrisburg.

1836: The Harrisburg Anti-Slavery Society is founded by about a hundred men and women. The first train rolls into the city, operated by the Harrisburg, Portsmouth, Mount Joy, and Lancaster Railroad. The city soon became, and long remained, a major rail center.

1837: The city's first railroad station is built.

1838: The "Buckshot War" occurred in December. Governor Ritner calls out state troops to stifle the political squabble. The first railroad sleeping car is built in Chambersburg and used on the route to Harrisburg.

1839: The rebuilt Zion Lutheran Church is the site of the Whig party's national convention, which nominates William Henry Harrison. He wins the presidency but dies in 1840. The Cumberland Valley railroad bridge goes into service across the Susquehanna, just south of the Camelback bridge.

Market Street in the 1920s was crowded with automobiles, trolley cars and pedestrians. This was the busy city that Penn Harris was built to serve. (HSDC)

Children feed the pigeons on the Capitol grounds as straw-hatted mother watches, circa 1900. (HSDC)

1840: The Young Men's and Young Ladies' Total Abstinence Society of Harrisburg is activated. The abstinence refers to alcohol. The first large scale furnace operation in Harrisburg is started by Hunt & Son, who erect a rolling mill along the Pennsylvania Canal, near Second and Paxton Street.

1841: The first waterworks with pumping station is completed at Fourth and Front Streets. The two-year-old Cumberland Valley Railroad Bridge burns down, leaving a mile-long pile of ash and rubble. The city's first permanant theater building, Shakespeare Hall, is built at Locust and Court Streets.

1843: Spofford's *Harrisburg Directory* stated that city brewers produced 465,000 gallons of beer and ale that year.

1844: The Central Division of the Sons of Temperance is organized in Harrisburg by over 200 men.

1845: Dauphin Deposit Bank opens. Harrisburg Cemetery established.

1846: The Camelback Bridge is half destroyed by flood.

1847: Frederick Douglass and William Lloyd Garrison hold an anti-slavery rally at the Dauphin County Court House in Harrisburg. Both are harrassed by the crowd.

1849: Construction of the first railroad bridge at Rockville.

1850: The Porter Furnace is established as the first anthracite furnace in Harrisburg.

According to the census, Harrisburg has 7,834 persons living in 1,376 dwellings. Harrisburg Gas Company begins operation.

1851: The State Lunatic Hospital is founded, one of the largest institutions in Harrisburg in its time.

1852: Harrisburg Cotton Manufacturing Company operates at Front and North Streets, present site of the YMCA. A co-educational high school opens at Capitol and Forster Streets on the site of the old city reservoir.

1853: Pennsylvania Female College offers classes in the John Harris Mansion. Central Iron Works established in south Harrisburg.

1854: The *Pennsylvania Patriot*, successor to the *Democratic Union* and ancestor of

The river seen here as viewed from the Capitol. State Street running from the Capitol to Front Street once looked like the Mall in Washington D.C. (HSDC)

the Harrisburg *Patriot-News*, begins publication. Harrisburg National Bank built on Market Square. The YMCA is founded as a public reading room with a small library. The Pennsylvania Railroad from Harrisburg to Pittsburgh is finished.

1855: The Reformed Jewish congregation is organized; a few years later it purchases the old Methodist church at the corner of Second and South Streets. The fortress-looking Dauphin County Prison is erected downtown, on Walnut Street behind the county court house.

1856: The Flash Boat Club is established.

1857: The Swatara Furnace, also known as the McCormick Furnace, is built at

Union Deposit in South Hanover Township. A much larger railroad station is built.

1858: The first train on the Reading Railroad comes puffing into Harrisburg on January 18, the day of the inauguration of Governor Pollock.

1859: Construction of the Reading station completed.

Pine Street Presbyterian Church opens for worship.

1860: Harrisburg incorporated as a city. The Market Square Presbyterian Church dedicated. The Broad Street Market opens for business.

1861: The Street Railway Company operates the first horse car. The line runs on Third Street from Walnut to Broad. From the Washington House hotel on February 22, President-elect Abraham Lincoln starts on his ride to Washington for his first inauguration. Camp Curtin established on the Dauphin county Fair Grounds. It becomes one of the largest military training sites of the Civil War.

1862: The First Baptist Church in Harrisburg is dedicated. Serves as a hospital for Confederates wounded in the battle of Gettysburg.

1863: Fort Washington was built on the west shore when the Union feared the Confederate army would not be stopped at Gettysburg. On June 30, Confederate forces

were met in Camp Hill by General Joseph Knipe's troops. After the engagement, units are raised to defend Harrisburg. Simon Cameron purchases the Harris Mansion.

1864: Lochiel Rolling Mill founded by Simon and J. Donald Cameron, makes rails for trains.

1865: Flood. March 18th. 24.6 feet.

1866: The Pennsylvania Steel company is organized in Steelton. Chesapeake Nail Works started by the Bailey brothers. The Camelback bridge is damaged by a spectacular fire.

1867: Highspire was incorporated as a borough, and its incorporation was annulled the very next year.

1869: The Paxton Rolling Mills are erected. Historical Society of Dauphin County organized. One of the oldest in the country.

1870: The first United Brethren Church in Harris-

Skyline showing Susquehanna River, bridges and Harrisburg. The river was and remains a recreation center. (HSDC)

Harrisburg's Art Deco skyscraper, the Harrisburger Hotel and the Payne Shoemaker Building, are seen from the terrace in front of the Capitol, circa 1940. (HSDC)

burg is erected. Services conducted in German.

1873: The horse-drawn Passenger Railway Company is incorporated. Harrisburg Grand Opera House opens. Harrisburg Hospital organized. The Lochiel Furnace is built by the Paxton Furnace Company. Located in south Harrisburg just north of Cedar Street along Paxton Creek.

1877: The new plant of the Central Iron Works is built by Charles L. Bailey. Located next to the river near South Front and Sycamore Streets. City troops guard the arsenal during the nation-wide railway strike.

1878: Telephones installed in Harrisburg.

1880: Steelton incorporated. The first lighting plant in Harrisburg—one of the first in the U.S.—was established under Thomas Edison's supervision.

1882: The Wednesday Club of Harrisburg, the first permanent musical organiza-

tion in Harrisburg and also the oldest in the country, is organized.

1885: Harrisburg's Centennial celebration lasted four days. There are 250 phone subscribers in Harrisburg.

1886: The first paved street is Strawberry, from Third Street to Market Square. Harrisburg Chamber of Commerce, also known as the Board of Trade, is chartered and opened.

1887: Another new railroad station is built, on the same site as the first two. A new Cumberland Valley Railroad bridge is completed.

1888: On July 4, the first trolley car runs between Harrisburg and Steelton.

1889: The last market day on Market Square is held on January 19, and then the Market houses are torn down. The first well-documented flood, occurred on June 2nd. 26.8 feet. E. Z. Wallower constructs the People's Bridge, now the Walnut Street Bridge.

1890: The Harris Park School, next to the river, admits its first pupils. The Harrisburg city library opens on Market Square, with about 3,000 volumes on its shelves.

1891: The first Mulberry Street bridge is completed, which stimulates building on Allison Hill.

1892: End of the horse-drawn trolley.

1893: The Dauphin Building rises, the first office building in Harrisburg. The Central High school opens for both boys and girls. Later becomes the girls' high school.

1894: Flood. May 22nd. 25.7 feet.

1895: The first synagogue of the Chisuk Emuna congregation is built on Filbert Street between State and North.

1897: The State Capitol Building burns down.

1898: The Harrisburg Civic Club, advocate of municipal progress, is organized by Mrs. Lyman Gilbert, premier activist. The Seiler School for girls opens. It merges with the Harrisburg Academy fifty years later. A special census identifies 33 ethnic groups in Steelton.

1900: Mira Lloyd Dock speaks to the Chamber of Commerce, calling for modern improvements and beautification in the city.

1901: The Pennsylvania Canal is vacated.

1902: Flood destroys portions of the Camelback bridge. March 3rd. 22.9 feet. The bridge is torn down the next year and replaced. James Kline drives the first automobile in the city. The Rockville stone bridge is completed north of Harrisburg. Vance McCormick elected Mayor of Harrisburg on a reform ticket. The "City Beautiful" movement will start soon. Vance McCormick purchases *The Patriot* newspaper company and competes against Edward J. Stackpole's Harrisburg *Telegraph*. The water filter plant is in operation on Hargest's (now City) Island. Because it provides an abundant, dependable supply of clean, pure water, citizens no longer have to drink from, or bathe in, the Susquehanna.

1903: Milton Hershey begins planning his chocolate factory, and the town of Hershey to go with it.

Civil War re-enactors mass at the Capitol in October 1997. The two wooden booths in front of the building are temporary shelters to house artisans at work restoring the famed Barnard statuary. Courtesy, City of Harrisburg, Stephen Reed, Mayor

1904: 100 passenger trains are stopping in the city each day. The Technical High School for boys is opened.

1905: The Lochiel Train Wreck. The Pennsylvania Railroad's Cleveland Express collided at Steelton with a freight train carrying dynamite. Twenty-two died, 130 were injured. Opening of the Bijou, the city's first motion picture theater. The United Trust Company Building goes up; six stories high, the city's first skyscraper. Harrisburg celebrates Old Home Week, attracting thousands of former residents.

1906: St. Michael's Lutheran Church opens. Services in German. The grand, new State Capitol Building is completed. President Theodore Roosevelt speaks at the dedication. The architect eventually goes to prison for fraud.

1907: Hersheypark opens. B'nai Jacob Synagogue opens in Middletown, the oldest synagogue building in Dauphin County. The new St. Patrick's Cathedral on State Street is completed and dedicated.

1909: Harrisburg Grand Opera House destroyed in a fiery conflagration.

1910: Scenic Bellevue Park laid out. Central Pennsylvania's first planned neighborhood.

1911: The Rotary Club, the first service club, is organized.

1912: Construction begins on the great cement river walk and steps that will run the five-mile length of the city.

1914: The new Harrisburg city library opens.

1916: The first Annual Kipona celebration takes place at

The major extension of the Capitol along with other new construction contributes to downtown's new cosmopolitan look. Courtesy, City of Harrisburg, Stephen Reed, Mayor

the riverside. The Indian name, meaning "bright or sparkling waters," was suggested by Dr. Hugh Hamilton. Bethlehem Steel takes over the Pennsylvania Steel Company plant in Steelton.

1917: St. Lawrence Catholic Church established for German Catholics. The *Evening News* begins publication. Olmsted Air Force Base is established near Middletown.

1919: Harrisburg Tech claims the national high school football championship, out-scoring its opponents 701-0.

1920: Ohev Sholom, the temple of the Reformed Jewish congregation, is completed at Front and Seneca Streets.

1921: Island Park's bathing beach has 235,000 spectators and bathers the first year.

1924: WHP, the first radio station in Harrisburg, begins broadcasting.

1926: Harrisburg Tech and Central High Schools close, to be replaced by William Penn and John Harris. Harrisburg Art Association formed. Polyclinic Hospital, organized in 1915, moves into its new complex.

1927: Rite Aid starts as a small Harrisburg grocery business; today one of the largest drug store chains in America.

1930: Bishop McDevitt Catholic High School opens.

1931: The YMCA erects its ornate headquarters and combination gymnasium, hotel, etc., on Front Street. State Farm Show complex built. Harrisburg Symphony Orchestra first plays.

1933: The opulent Hotel Hershey opens.

1936: Another flood. Worst so far. March 19th. 29.2 feet.

1937: Chocolate workers' strike in Hershey is fiercely ended by neighboring dairy farmers.

1938: Capital Blue Cross, the health insurer, is organized by the city's hospitals and physicians. Buses replace trolleys in the city.

1941: Mountain water first piped to the city from De-Hart Dam in Clarks Valley.

1943: U. A. Whitaker moves the headquarters of Aircraft-Marine Products (simply AMP today) to Harrisburg. Becomes the world's leading producer of electrical/electronic connection devices. The new Dauphin County Courthouse opens. Its neo-classical, Art Deco style, designed by Lawrie and Green, still looks fresh.

1947: Merchants and Business Men's Mutual Insurance Company moves to occupy the splendid King mansion on Front Street.

1948: The Harrisburg *Telegraph* shuts down.

1949: John O'Hara's latest novel *A Rage to Live* is set in Harrisburg. Pennsylvania National Insurance Group moves to its new headquarters at 19th and Derry Streets.

1950: 89,554 people live in Harrisburg.

The interior of the recently restored Broad Street Market provides a culturally diverse shopping experience. Courtesy, City of Harrisburg, Stephen Reed, Mayor

Residential construction along North Second Street in the 1990s is a sure sign that there is a renewed interest in living in the city. Courtesy, City of Harrisburg, Stephen Reed, Mayor

1952: Nationwide Insurance expands its office complex on Derry Street. The Harvey Taylor bridge opens and speeds traffic between the city and the west shore.

1954: The Shiremanstown Quaker Oats plant gears up.

1956: Phoenix Steel (formerly Central Iron and Steel) is leveled to make way for the Interstate 83 bridge. Two years later about 150 houses in Shipoke will be taken down.

1958: IBM builds a branch of its Field Engineering Division at Mechanicsburg. The new distribution center is completed in 1982.

1959: The Harrisburg Academy moves to Wormleysburg on the west shore.

1960: An imposing stone house at 311-313 North Front Street is torn down, for a parking lot. It was the former Governor's Mansion. The John Harris Bridge (popularly known as the 83 or South Bridge) opens for traffic across the river.

1960s: The Olmsted Air Force Base closes, but Penn State University would establish its Capitol Campus at the site (now Penn State at Harrisburg, Capital College).

1963: Harrisburg Area Community College chartered. The new campus opens in Wildwood Park north of the city in 1967.

1964: The modern State Museum and Archives buildings are completed in the Capitol complex.

1965: The Pennsylvania Medical Society moves to the west shore.

1966: Penn State's Milton S. Hershey Medical Center, with medical school, opens in Hershey.

1972: Hersheypark undergoes major remodeling. Hurricane Agnes produces Harrisburg's very worst flood.

June 24th. 32.6 feet. The capital made headlines as the site of the "Harrisburg 7" trial. Anti-war radicals were found innocent of plotting to kidnap government officials.

1973: E. Z. Wallower's Penn Harris Hotel, once the pride of Harrisburg, is torn down. Historic Harrisburg Association is formed. Often mistaken for a historical society, its mission is downtown preservation

1974: A new Commonwealth National Bank is built at Market Square on the site of the old Harrisburg National Bank, built in 1854.

1976: Broad Street Market restored.

1977: Strawberry Square shopping and office complex opens on the former site of the Penn Harris Hotel.

1978: Redevelopment and restoration begin in Shipoke.

1979: Three Mile Island Nuclear Plant accident.

1980: Harrisburg, population down from 90,000 to 53,000, is listed as the second-most distressed city in the nation.

1981: Stephen Reed is elected Mayor of Harrisburg.

New City Government Center built at Market Square.

1983: Pennsylvania Blue Shield's new headquarters complex is completed in Camp Hill. Now the largest Blue Shield plan in the country, with more than 2,000 employees. AMP locates its new headquarters next to the Harrisburg East Mall.

1984: Harrisburg awarded the title "All-American City" by the National Municipal League.

1985: Pennsylvania Hospital Insurance Company (PHICO) opens its prize-winning headquarters building in Silver Spring township.

1986: The city's refurbished train station wins a top historic preservation award.

Strawberry Square, completed in the 1990s incorporates historic facades in its shopping arcade. Courtesy, City of Harrisburg, Stephen Reed, Mayor

Capitol's east wing plaza completed.

1987: Redevelopment of City Island begins, with RiverSide Stadium its centerpiece, where the Harrisburg Senators baseball team will play.

1990: Harrisburg is named an All-American City for the second time. The Harrisburg Hilton and Towers opens on Market Square. The city has its downtown hotel. Italian Lake spruced up. The Walnut Street Bridge is festooned with lights.

1991: Reservoir Park restored and improved.

1996: Construction on the Whitaker Center for Science and the Arts begins downtown on the site of the former Pomeroy's department store. Walnut Street Bridge collapses as river crests at 20 feet. Fire destroys homes at Pancake Row.

1997: Penn National Insurance moves its headquarters from Derry Street to a new high rise on Market Square.

1998: Sylvan Heights mansion overlooking the city is refurbished by the YWCA and becomes their new headquarters. Includes the Kunkel Center for Women and Children. Stephen Reed begins his record fifth term as Mayor.

Strawberry Square, the Locust Street Parking Garage and the Hilton Hotel are linked by a glassed overpass. The overpass also serves as an extension of the Strawberry Square food court and is a popular place to have lunch and people-watch. Courtesy, City of Harrisburg, Stephen Reed, Mayor

1998: "Restaurant Row" starts with the opening of Fire House and Stock's on Second.

1999: Whitaker Center for Science and the Arts completes construction.

2000: State legislature passes bill giving control of Harrisburg Schools to Mayor Reed. Crowne Plaza Hotel opens.

2001: National Civil War Museum opens in Reservoir Park. Midtown Cinema established.

2002: Harrisburg High wins the AAAA State Basketball championship. Farm Show Arena expands. Hershey Trust considers the sale of Hershey Foods but backs off after local opposition.

2003: Mayor Reed's Old West Museum plans and artifact purchases revealed. City's crime rate among highest in Pennsylvania, school test scores among lowest.

2005: Harrisburg University of Science and Technology opens. Salary.com ranks Harrisburg as one of the best cities in which to work and live, and Kipplinger's ranks region 12th best in nation

2006: Construction begins on the Harrisburg University downtown tower. Mayor Stephen R. Reed marks his 25th year in office

2007: Controversy erupts between the city and federal governments on the location of the proposed Federal Courthouse. City Council forces Mayor Reed to sell Old West Museum artifacts. The Spot cafe shuts down 2008: City begins preparations for "SusqueCentennial" 150th anniversary celebration.

2008: Harrisburg Roman Catholic Diocese announces that Bishop McDevitt High School will move out of the city. Presidential candidate Barak Obama charms Harrisburg with his visit in April, but rival Hillary Clinton wins the Democratic Pennsylvania primary.

2009: "Shocker!" exclaimed *The Patriot-News* on Wednesday, May 20, 2009. In the previous day's primary election, City Council President Linda D. Thompson had upset Harrisburg's "Mayor for Life" Stephen R. Reed.

BIBLIOGRAPHY

Published Sources

Allen, Jean Gray. "One Hundred Stepping Stones, 1860-1960, Harrisburg Centennial." In *Harrisburg Centennial Celebration, 1860-1960* (Official Program). Harrisburg, Pa.: n.p., 1960, pp. 15-35.

Ayres, George Bucher. "The Burning of John Harris. Reeder's Painting." *Papers of the Historical Society of Dauphin County*, vol. 1, n.d., pp. 37-41.

Beers, Paul. *Profiles from the Susquehanna Valley*. Harrisburg, Pa.: Stackpole Books, 1973.

———. *Pennsylvania Politics, Today and Yesterday; The Tolerable Accommodation*. University Park, Pa.: Pennsylvania State University Press, 1980.

Bell, Margaret Van Horn (Dwight). *A Journey to Ohio in 1810 as Recorded in the Journal of Margaret Van Horn Dwight*. Ed. Max Farrand. New Haven: Yale University Press, 1912.

Bigart, Homer. "A Quiet Setting for a Big Trial; Harrisburg Awaits Opening Today of Berrigan Case." *New York Times*, January 24, 1972, p. 12, col. 3.

Bodnar, John. "The Formation of Ethnic Consciousness: Slavic Immigrants in Steelton." In *The Ethnic Experience in Pennsylvania*. Ed. Bodnar. Lewisburg, Pa.: Bucknell University Press, 1973, pp. 309-330.

———. *Immigration and Industrialization: Ethnicity in an American Mill Town, 1870-1940*. Pittsburgh: University of Pittsburgh Press, 1977.

Book, Janet Mae. *Northern Rendezvous*. Harrisburg, Pa.: Telegraph Press, 1951.

Boyer, Richard, and David Savageau. *Places Rated Almanac*. Chicago: Rand McNally, 1981

Cochran, Thomas C. *Pennsylvania; A Bicentennial History*. New York: W.W. Norton, 1978.

Coleman, Michael B. *The Jews of Harrisburg, An Informal History by a Native Son*. Harrisburg, Pa.: privately published, 1978.

Constitution, By-Laws, and Rules of Order, of Central Division, No. 10, of the Sons of Temperance, of the State of Pennsylvania. Harrisburg, Pa.: J.A. Spofford, 1845.

Dauphin County Historical Review. Vol. 1, 1952-Vol. 14, 1966.

Davis, Amelia, Carl Oblinger, and David McBride, eds. *Glimpses into Our Lives: Memories of Harrisburg's Black Senior Citizens*. Harrisburg, Pa.: Pennsylvania Historical and Museum Commission, 1978.

Day, Dorothy. "Tale of Two Capitals." *Commonweal*, July 14, 1939, pp. 289-290.

Dewitt, William R. *Profanity and Intemperance, Prevailing Evils*. Harrisburg, Pa.: Fenn and Wallace, 1840. Printed for the Young Men's and Young Ladies' Total Abstinence Society of Harrisburg.

Dill, Malcolm H. *Planning for the Future of the Harrisburg Area; Report of the Harrisburg Area Regional Planning Committee of the Municipal League of Harrisburg, Pennsylvania*. Harrisburg, Pa.: Municipal League of Harrisburg, 1940.

Donehoo, George P. *Harrisburg, The City Beautiful, Romantic, and Historic*. Harrisburg, Pa.: Telegraph Press, 1927.

Egle, William Henry. "Old Times and Old People." *Papers of the HSDC*, vol. 2, n.d., pp. 75-103.

———. *History of the Counties of Dauphin and Lebanon in the Commonwealth of Pennsylvania: Biographical and Genealogical*. Philadelphia: Everts and Peck, 1883.

———, ed. *Centenary Memorial of the Erection of the County of Dauphin and the Founding of the City of Harrisburg*. Harrisburg, Pa.: Telegraph Printing House, 1886.

First Annual Report of the Board of Trustees of the State Lunatic Hospital of the State of Pennsylvania. Harrisburg, Pa.: Theo. Fenn and Co., 1852.

Frew, Ken. "Tales From 'Pancake Row.'" *Harrisburg Heritage; Monthly Newsletter of the Historic Harrisburg Association, Inc.* August, 1978, pp. 1-5.

Garraty, John. *The American Nation*. 2 vols., 3rd ed. New York: Harper and Row, 1975

Harrisburg; A Walk Through History. Harrisburg, Pa.: Harrisburg Branch, American Association of University Women, and Historic Harrisburg Association, 1981.

Harrisburg, Pennsylvania, As Seen by the Carrier Boys of Harrisburg's Greatest Home Newspaper, the Daily Telegraph. Harrisburg, Pa.: Telegraph Press, 1904.

Harrisburg, Pennsylvania Industrial Survey, Harrisburg Chamber of Commerce, 1928.

Hiler, Jean. "Dr. John Curwen and Victorian Psychiatry in Pennsylvania." M.A. Thesis, Pennsylvania State University, Capitol Campus, 1981.

Huston, Ralph D. *No—Back and Over*. Privately published, 1975.

Inglewood, Marian. *Then and Now in Harrisburg*. Harrisburg, Pa.: n.p., 1925.

Keefer, Horace Andrew. "Early Iron Industries in Dauphin County." *Publications of the Dauphin County Historical Society*, 1927

Kelker, Luther Reily. *History of Dauphin County*. 3 vols. New York: Lewis Pub. Co., 1907.

Klein, Philip S., and Ari Hoogenboom. *A History of Pennsylvania*. 2nd ed. University Park, Pa.: Pennsylvania

State University Press, 1980.

Klein, Theodore. "Hot Times in Harrisburg; The Fire Boys from 1837-1871." *Papers of the Historical Society of Dauphin County*, vol. 1, n.d., pp. 61-71.

———. "East Market Street When I Was a Boy." *Papers of the Historical Society of Dauphin County*, vol. 1, n.d., pp. 23-33.

Laverty, George Lauman. *History of Medicine in Dauphin County Pennsylvania*.

Lewis, C. *Temperance. Lecture Delivered in the Lochiel Church, Saturday, February 6, 1869*. Harrisburg, Pa.: Sieg, pr. State Guard, 1869.

Maclay, William. *The Journal of William Maclay*. 1890; rpt. New York: Albert and Charles Boni, 1927.

Milspaw, Yvonne J. "Folklore and the Nuclear Age: The Harrisburg Disaster at Three Mile Island." *International Folklore Review*, 1 (1981), pp. 57-65.

Morgan, George H. *Annals of Harrisburg.* rev. ed. by L. Frances Morgan Black. n.p. 1906.

Myers, Richmond E. *The Long Crooked River*. Boston: Christopher Publishing House, 1949.

Orwig, J.R. *The Harrisburg Visitors' Guide, 1876, for the Use of Strangers Visiting the City*. Harrisburg, Pa.: Patriot Publishing Co., 1876.

Pardoe, Hiles C. *Up the Susquehanna*. New York: Hunt and Eaton, 1895.

Patriot, The (Harrisburg)

Polk's Greater Harrisburg City Directory. Vol. 70. Boston: R.L. Polk, 1946.

Prolix, Peregrine. (pseud.) *Journey Through Pennsylvania—1835—By Canal, Rail and Stage Coach.* Intro. William H. Shank. 1836; rpt. York, Pa.: American Canal and Transportation Center, 1975.

Proposed Municipal Improvements for Harrisburg, Pa.; Report of the Executive Committee to Subscribers to Fund for Investigating Municipal Improvements, Nov. 21, 1901. n.p.

Report of the Trustees and Superintendent of the State Lunatic Hospital of Pennsylvania, 1858. Harrisburg, Pa.: A. Boyd Hamilton, 1859.

Rupp, I. Daniel. *The History and Topography of Dauphin, Cumberland, Franklin, Bedford, Adams, and Perry Counties.* Lancaster, Pa.: Gilbert Hills, 1846.

Schulman, Jay, Phillip Shaver, Robert Colman, Barbara Emrich, and Richard Christie. "Recipe For a Jury."
Psychology Today, May 1973, pp. 37-44, 77-84.

Snavely, Joseph Richard. *The Story of Hershey, The Chocolate Town.* Hershey, Pa.: n.p., 1953

J.A. Spofford's Harrisburg Directory for 1843. Harrisburg, Pa.: J.A. Spofford, 1843.

Stamm, A.C. "The Progress of Harrisburg." *Publications of the Historical Society of Dauphin County.* April 15, 1935.

Steinmetz, G.M., and Robert Hammond Murray. *Twenty-five Years of Service; The Penn Harris Hotel.* Harrisburg, Pa.: Telegraph Press, 1943.

Steinmetz, Richard, Sr., and Robert Hoffsommer. *This Was Harrisburg.* Harrisburg, Pa.: Stackpole Books, 1976.

Stevens, Sylvester K. *Pennsylvania, Birthplace of a Nation.* New York: Random House, 1964.

Sunday Patriot-News (Harrisburg), "82 Newcomers Guide," September 19, 1982.

Tocqueville, Alexis de. *Democracy in America.* Ed. Phillips Bradley. New York: Vintage Books, 1945.

Trautmann, Frederick, ed. "Pennsylvania Through a German's Eyes: The Travels of Ludwig Gall, 1819-1820." *Pennsylvania Magazine of History and Biography*, 105 (January 1981), pp. 35-65.

U.S. Immigration Commission. *Reports of the U.S.I.C.: Immigrants in Industries, Part 2: Iron and Steel*, 2 vols. S. Doc. 633, 61st Cong. 2nd Sess. Serial 5669 (1911), pp. 630-659.

Urdang, Laurence. Ed. *The Timetables of American History.* New York: Simon and Schuster, 1981.

Wilson, William H. " 'More Almost Than the Men': Mira Lloyd Dock and the Beautification of Harrisburg." *Pennsylvania Magazine of History and Biography*, 99 (October 1975), pp. 490-499.

———. "Harrisburg's Successful City Beautiful Movement, 1900-1915." *Pennsylvania History*, 47 (July 1980), pp. 213-233.

Woodside, Robert E. *My Life and Town.* Millersburg, Pa.: n.p., 1979.

Unpublished Sources

Africa, Mrs. Benjamin F. "A Century Ago—Harrisburg and its Residents, As Described by Anne Royall." Lecture, Historical Society of Dauphin County (hereafter HSDC), December 19, 1932. TS.

Allen, Jean Gray. Scrapbooks of Harrisburg newspaper clippings, 1957-59, 1961. HSDC.

Bowman, A.M., comp. "Narratives Regarding the Northern March of the Confederates During the War of the Rebellion." Folder No. 2, TI-7. Dull Collection. HSDC. TS.

"Constitution of the Anti-Slavery Society of Harrisburg, 1836." HSDC. MS.

Crist, R.W. "Harrisburg and the War Effort." Lecture, HSDC, September 20, 1943. TS.

Demming, Col. Henry C. "Reminiscences of Harrisburg During the 60's." Lecture, HSDC, December 14, 1922. TS.

———. Letter to Casper Dull, October 15, 1900. Folder No. 4, TI-9. Dull Collection. HSDC. TS.

Detweiler, Bertha Hoffer, comp. Scrapbooks of Harrisburg Newspaper Clippings, 1926-1945. Nos. 1, 5, 9, 11, 15, 28. HSDC.

Drawbaugh, Allen. (sic) Scrapbooks of Notes on Steelton. HSDC. TS.

"For 'Tippecanoe and Tyler Too': The Whig National Convention at Harrisburg." Lecture, HSDC, n.d. TS.

Gorgas, William L. Statement on Confederate Invasion of Pennsylvania. Folder No. 3, TI-8. Dull Collection. HSDC. TS.

Gross, Col. Henry. "Reminiscences of Early Harrisburg." Lecture, HSDC, June 16, 1958. TS.

Hamilton, A. Boyd. Scrapbooks of Harrisburg Newspaper Clippings, 1912, 1935-1938. HSDC.

"The Harrisburg Anti-Slavery Society." Lecture, HSDC, December 1911. MS.

Harrisburg League for Municipal Improvements. Scrapbook, 1902. HSDC.

Keller, J.P. "Personal Recollections. A Few Leading Events in Harrisburg 50 Years Ago." Lecture, HSDC, c1896. MS.

———. "Personal Recollections of Earlier Days in Harrisburg." Lecture, HSDC, May 9, 1901. MS.

———. "As Others See Us." Lecture, HSDC, June 14, 1906. TS.

Kunkle, Dr. Beverly Waugh. "Genetic (sic) and Geneology of Front Street." Lecture, HSDC, October 1967. TS.

Liebman, Caroline, comp. Data From Patient Records, State Lunatic Hospital of Pennsylvania, Harrisburg,

Pa., 1851-1874. MS in author's possession.

Malmsheimer, Lonna. "And You Were Worried About the Bomb? Image, Fiction, and Frame in the Three-Mile Island Emergency." TS in author's possession.

Miller, Evan J. "When the Circus Came to Harrisburg." Lecture, HSDC, May 18, 1981. TS.

Miller, Herman P. "Early Recollections." Lecture, HSDC, n.d. TS.

Milspaw, Yvonne, and Julius Kassovic. "A Folklorist Perspective on the Three Mile Island Accident." TS in author's possession.

Pearson, William, Sr. "My Early Recollections of Front Street Between Mulberry and Walnut Streets." Lecture, HSDC, n.d. TS.

Rutherford, D.I. "Reminiscences of the War: Capt. James Elder's Company in the Emergency of 1862." Lecture, HSDC, n.d. TS.

Settino, David Lee. "Steelton's Cultural Development." TS in author's possession.

Simonton, Mrs. John (Sallie). Diary, March 16-18, 1865. HSDC. MS.

Simonton, William. "Notes on My Recollections of Country Life in West Hanover Township, Dauphin County, Pennsylvania, in the Thirties of the Nineteenth Century, 1904." HSDC. MS.

Stoner, Carl B., Sr. "Between Shipoke and Goat Town." Lecture, HSDC, March 14, 1966. TS.

Swallow, Rev. Silas C. "The Susquehanna—Navigable Yet Unnavigable." Lecture, HSDC, March 11, 1915. MS.

Wallower, E.Z. "Reminiscences of Old Harrisburg." Lecture, HSDC, November 1930. TS.

Warfel, Stephen G. "The Prehistory of Dauphin County, Pennsylvania." Lecture, HSDC, October 20, 1980. TS.

Weitzel, Walter M. "Some History and Use of the Susquehanna." Lecture, HSDC, June 15, 1931. TS.

Young, R.I. Diary, June 22-July 5, 1863. HSDC. MS.

WAKE UP! THEY'RE LOOKING AT YOU

Additional *Harrisburg Moving Road* bibliography

Published Sources:
Barton, Michael, and Simon Bronner. *Steelton.* Charleston, SC: Arcadia Publishing, 2008.
Barton, Michael, and Jessica Dorman. *Harrisburg's Old Eighth Ward.* Charleston, S.C.: Arcadia Publishing, 2002.
Barton, Michael, ed. *Susquehanna Heritage: A Journal of the Historical Society of Dauphin County*, 1 (Fall, 2002), Special Inaugural Issue, "The McCormicks of Harrisburg."
———."Almost Our Own Montmartre: Studying Harrisburg's Old Eighth Ward." *Pennsylvania History*, 72 (Autumn, 2005), pp. 405-418.
———."Doing Time in Dauphin County, 1842-1901," *Pennsylvania Heritage*, Fall, 1984, pp. 4-9.
Crist, Robert Grant. *Camp Hill: A History.* Camp Hill, Pa.: Plank's Suburban Press, 1985.
———.*Harrisburg Hospital: The First Hundred Years, 1873-1973.* Harrisburg, Pa.: Harrisburg Hospital, 1973.
Eggert, Gerald. *Harrisburg Industrializes: The Coming of Factories to an American Community.* University Park, Pa.: Pennsylvania State University Press, 1993.

Houts, Mary Davidoff, and Pamela Cassidy Whiteneck, *Hershey.* Charleston, S.C.: Arcadia Publishing, 2000.
Morrison, Ernest. *The City on the Hill: A History of the Harrisburg State Hospital.* Harrisburg, Pa.: n. p., 1992.
———. *J. Horace McFarland: A Thorn for Beauty.* Harrisburg, Pa.: Pennsylvania Historical and Museum Commission, 1995.
Richman, Irwin. *The Pennsylvania Dutch Country.* Charleston, S.C.: Arcadia Publishing, 2004.
Ries, Linda. *Harrisburg.* Charleston, S.C.: Arcadia Publishing, 2000.
Scott, John Weldon, and Eric Ledell Smith. *African Americans of Harrisburg.* Charleston, S.C.: Arcadia Publishing, 2005.
Stuart, Jeb. *Harrisburg PA: An Economic and Community Profile.* Harrisburg: Journal Publications, 2009.
Wallower, E. Z. *Reminiscences of E. Z. Wallower.* Harrisburg, Pa.: n. p., 1941.
Wilson, William H. *The City Beautiful Movement.* Baltimore: Johns Hopkins University Press, 1989.

Unpublished Sources
Frew, Ken. Building Harrisburg: The Architects and Builders, 1719-1941. TS in author's possession.

Stuart, Jeb. The Harrisburg History Project. Commissioned by Mayor Stephen R. Reed. TS in author's possession.

Websites
http://www.old8thward.com Harrisburg's Old Eighth Ward, An Urban Social History Project of Penn State Harrisburg's American Studies Program. Produced by Michael Barton, Webmaster, Stephanie Patterson Gilbert.
http://www.hbg.psu.edu/hum/ McCormick/index2.htm The McCormick Family Papers. A Social History and Culture Studies Project of the Center for Pennsylvania Culture Studies. Produced by Michael Barton, Webmaster, MaryAlice Bitts.
http://www.rawnjournals.com Faithful Hand: The Journals of Charles Coatesworth Pinckney Rawn, 1830-1865 . . . . A Project of the Historical Society of Dauphin County and Penn State Harrisburg's American Studies Program and Center for Pennsylvania Culture. Studies. Produced by Michael Barton. Webmaster, Stephen Bachmann.

Index